FREE LOVE

FREE LOVE

THE STORY OF A GREAT AMERICAN SCANDAL

ROBERT SHAPLEN

WITH A FOREWORD BY LOUIS MENAND

McNally Editions

New York

McNally Editions
134 Prince St.
New York, NY 10012

ISBN: 978-1-946022-91-2
E-book: 978-1-961341-00-5

Design by Jonathan Lippincott

1   3   5   7   9   10   8   6   4   2

For Marti

FOREWORD

On an elegant residential block in Brooklyn Heights stands what once may have been the most famous church in America. The Plymouth Church, on Hicks Street, was founded in 1847 with just twenty-one members. The businessmen who established it, Congregationalists in a Presbyterian town, wanted it to grow, so they offered the job of minister to a man named Henry Ward Beecher, thanks to whose preaching prowess the Second Presbyterian Church in Indianapolis had become the largest congregation in the city. Beecher accepted the offer. He would preach at Plymouth Church for the next forty years, eventually to full houses of two thousand worshippers of the Christian god.

Beecher was a legend in his own time. Manhattanites took special ferries, referred to as Beecher Boats, across the East River to hear his sermons. John Hay, Abraham Lincoln's private secretary, later Secretary of State, called him "the greatest preacher the world has seen since Saint Paul preached on Mars Hill."

In nineteenth-century America, sermons were a widely diffused entertainment medium. People bought print collections of sermons, but the sermon itself was essentially performance art. It was not so much what was said, though sometimes doctrinal disputes were litigated by dueling ministers. Sermons were intended to do more than persuade. They were designed to excite, to thrill, to move.

Reading sermons in a book therefore gives us little idea of the kind of effect they had on their listeners. In Beecher's day, the sermons was increasingly ad-libbed. Beecher would bring notes onto the stage, but he treated them as props. He would toss them on the floor or on a table and hold forth as he strode back and forth before the congregation.

Beecher's father, Lyman, himself a noted preacher, was a Calvinist, but Henry preached what become known as the Gospel of Love, a theology that might be encapsulated in the question, Is it a sin to feel that I am sinless? Beecher asked parishioners to receive God's love through Jesus Christ and taught that this form of religious belief is consistent with the enjoyment of life. Today, this seems a standard form of Christian evangelism, but in the nineteenth century it was revolutionary. It helped transform popular Protestantism from a religion obsessed with sin and damnation into what is essentially a mode of self-help. Love God and do what you like. The Word will set you free.

Beecher arrived in Brooklyn just as the nation was entering the final countdown to the Civil War. The conclusion of the Mexican War, in 1848, revived an issue that had been present at the Founding but had lain dormant since: whether slavery could or should by outlawed in the new territories. For the next twelve years, this question burned a hole in American political life. It defeated the democratic process. It was only settled by a war, in which six hundred thousand men died.

Beecher emerged as a leading antislavery spokesman, his prominence aided by the fact that the author of the best-selling book of the nineteenth century, a book Abraham Lincoln is supposed to have said caused the Civil War, *Uncle Tom's Cabin*, was his sister. The Fugitive Slave Act of 1850 permitted "slave catchers" to kidnap fugitives in free states and return them, without due process, to their owners, and Plymouth Church became a stop on the Underground Railroad. Fugitives hid out in its basement as they made their way to Canada. In 1856, when a call went out to send arms to "free-state" settlers who were battling "slave-state" settlers in Kansas, Beecher raised money from his congregation to send rifles. These were known as "Beecher's Bibles." More spectacularly, Beecher staged "slave auctions" in his church. He would locate slave owners looking to sell their property, bring the enslaved persons into the church, and, as they stood there, encourage parishioners to make offerings to purchase their freedom. The congregation was basically competing with slave traders for the "possession" of human beings.

The most famous of Beecher's slave auctions was of a nine-year-old girl named Pinky. Pinky was light-complexioned—the man selling her was likely her father, who had already sold the rest of her family to slave traders—and the congregation reportedly went wild when Beecher brought her on stage. Nine hundred dollars was collected, along with a gold ring, which Beecher dramatically placed on Pinky's finger. It was, he told her, her "freedom ring."

During the war, Beecher sponsored a regiment for the sons of parishioners, the First Long Island Regiment, known as "Beecher's Pets." And in 1863, the trustees of his church sent Beecher to England, where he spoke in Liverpool and Manchester, cities with textile industries dependent on cheap Southern cotton. Despite violent heckling, he kept his composure. Lincoln was impressed by the reports he heard, and he is supposed to have told his Cabinet that if the American flag was someday raised again over Fort Sumter, Beecher should be the one to do it, because "without Beecher in England there might have been no flag to raise." And in the event, Beecher was present.

Beecher's celebrity sold pews, and he was rewarded with a generous salary, which he supplemented by touring and giving talks. And he continued to promote social and political causes as part of his ministry, including women's suffrage. After the war, he was said to be the best-known minister in the United States.

Beecher did not preach like a theologian. He mixed his speeches with slang and jokes, and he seems to have had a palette of oratorical styles. He could be understated and matter-of-fact, but he was capable of magniloquence. Here is an excerpt from one of his earliest sermons, pre-Brooklyn, published in a popular collection called *Seven Lectures to Young Men*.

> The agony of midnight massacre, the phrenzy of the ship's dungeon, the living death of the middle passage, the wails of separation, the dismal torpor of hopeless servitude—are these found only in the piracy of the slave trade? They are all among us! worse assassinations! worse dragging to a prison-ship! worse groans ringing from the fetid hold! worse separation of families! worse bondage of intemperate men, enslaved by that most inexorable of all task-masters—sensual habit!

He seems to be referring to masturbation. If so, he soon dropped this displeasure with pleasure. Photographs make him look like a moony and slightly dissipated undergraduate, and rather corpulent when he was older, but his contemporaries described him as good-looking. He was not notably brilliant or even consistent intellectually, but he plainly had a charisma that made up for everything else. Rock stars are not usually consistent or intellectually impressive, either, but they are stars for a reason. And in nineteenth-century America, a celebrity minister was a kind of rock star.

Beecher therefore always had a female following (it could not have hurt that he preached the Gospel of Love), and rumors of affairs with parishioners date from his time in Indianapolis. In Brooklyn, two women confessed to their husbands that they had carried on affairs with Beecher. (Both husbands, strangely, were close to Beecher personally and professionally.) In 1872, the confession of one of those women became public. This led, three years later, to a lawsuit by the aggrieved husband, who accused Beecher of the tort of "criminal conversation" (a legalistic euphemism). The trial was the most sensational of the century.

As Reconstruction was falling apart in the South, newspaper readers were absorbed by the goings on in Tilton v. Beecher. In the six months leading up to the trial (which itself lasted six months), the *New York Times* published a hundred and five articles and thirty-seven editorials about the Beecher affair. People waited overnight in line to get seats in the courtroom. There were scalpers. Many colorful figures had walk-on roles in the story, from the feminists Victoria Woodhull and Elizabeth Cady Stanton to the manic Civil War general Benjamin Butler and the anti-pornography crusader Anthony Comstock.

Multiple cultural trends converged. The crackdown on obscenity, the Gospel of Love, feminism, above all, perhaps, the doctrine of free love promoted by Woodhull. That doctrine did not mean "love the one you're with" so much as "be with the one you love." If Beecher had fallen out of love with his wife and in love with Tilton's, all might be forgiven. The famous trial and the people and events surrounding it are the subject of Robert Shaplen's *Free Love and Heavenly Sinners*, the original title of the book you hold in your hands.

Shaplen was not a historian. He was a journalist who began his career in 1937 as a reporter for the *New York Herald Tribune*. In 1943, he became the Pacific War correspondent for *Newsweek*, and he landed with the marines at Leyte, in the Philippines, in 1944, the beginning of a long career reporting from Asia. He was with Mao in 1946 and he reported on Indonesia, Korea, and the French war in Indochina. When the United States entered the war in Vietnam, in 1965, he was one of the best-informed and most experienced reporters on that beat. He published ten books, most of them on Asia.

Free Love was originally a *New Yorker* article. Shaplen had written a few pieces for the magazine in the 1940s, including a piece on the Leyte invasion. In 1952, he became a staff writer, which he remained until his death, in 1988, at the age of seventy-one.

Nineteen fifty-two is a year well-known to *New Yorker* obsessives because it was the year that William Shawn became the magazine's editor. Shawn's taste in magazine writing was a shade more sober than his predecessor, Harold Ross (Ross had published John Hersey's "Hiroshima" in 1946, but the piece was commissioned by Shawn), and Shawn soon sent Shaplen back to Asia. Over much of the next four decades, Shaplen filed dispatches from all over the region—Burma, Manila, Hong Kong, Saigon, Bangkok, Algiers, Laos, Macao. Many were published as "Letters from," or under the magazine's semi-facetious rubric "Our Far-Flung Correspondents."

What drew Shaplen to the Beecher trial is a mystery, except that magazine writers, unlike scholars, are not specialists. They are writers. Professors plow the same furrow for forty years. Magazine writers write the stories they are assigned. When the magazine's needs change, so do the assignments.

It seems that Shaplen was either directed or encouraged to write on the Beecher trial by Shawn himself, and he approached the assignment in the spirit of the investigative reporter. He went to the original sources and, from them, produced this remarkably level-headed and absorbing account, a version of events consistent with much more recent, well-received treatments, Richard Wightman Fox's *Trials of Intimacy* (1999) and Debby Applegate's biography of Beecher, *The Most Famous Man in America*, which won a Pulitzer Prize in 2007.

Portions of Shaplen's book were serialized in the *New Yorker* and it was published, by Knopf, in 1954. (This was a custom at Shawn's *New Yorker* highly attractive to writers: they sold their work twice, first to the magazine, then to a publisher.) And stylistically, the book is very much old-*New-Yorker*. That style had a key element that distinguished it from most other magazine journalism. It was readable. That sounds banal, but actually it is not easy for many writers to produce prose that does not give work to the reader. When you are "assumptive"— that is, when you assume that readers will catch an allusion or a dropped name—you are making work for the reader. The old *New Yorker* edited the assumptiveness out. No one had to stop to puzzle out an allusion.

The old *New Yorker* also—and this is maybe a less worthy aspiration—believed in letting the facts speak for themselves. Writers were advised (I was advised, when I first started writing for the magazine, in 1990) not to have too many ideas. This was partly from a desire, again, not to make life difficult for the reader. But it was also a way of producing an effect of non-judgmental aloofness. This aloofness, not quite snobby but not without some hint of superiority, too, was part of the magazine's sensibility in the 1950s because it was an attitude to which its generally upscale readers aspired.

The non-judgmental, just-the-facts approach doesn't work for some subjects. Usually, the writer has to speak for the facts. But an air of bemused detachment works beautifully for the Beecher trial. The frenzy generated by the case seems incomprehensible today. Almost everyone involved comes off as comical or deranged, occasionally both. How could so much be thought to turn on the question of whether a man had sex with the wife of one of his friends? These things happened, even in Comstock-era America. Shaplen does not render a verdict, but he gives us the facts we need to reach our own.

Louis Menand
Cambridge, MA, 2024

PREFACE

In the writing of this book I have used original source material almost exclusively. The story of the famous scandal is told in narrative style, chronologically. Quotations and details of events culled from several score books, pamphlets, and newspapers have been used to recreate the dramatic story in its daily unfolding over a period of many years. My chief source has been the official record of the trial, a three-volume, three-thousand-page transcript of the case in City Court, Brooklyn, entitled *Theodore Tilton vs. Henry Ward Beecher, Action for Crim. Con.*, and published by McDivitt, Campbell & Co., in New York, in 1875. Of particular help in furnishing background material and guidance were the following: eight scrapbooks of clippings from the *Independent*, in the New York Public Library; *The True History of the Brooklyn Scandal*, by C. F. Marshall, published by the National Publishing Company, in Philadelphia, in 1874; *The Great Sensation*, by Leon Oliver, published by the Beverly Company, in Chicago, in 1873; *The Terrible Siren*, by Emanie Sachs, published by Harper & Bros., in New York, in 1928; *Henry Ward Beecher: An American Portrait*, by Paxton Hibben, published by George H. Doran and Company, in New York, in 1927; *Beecher and His Accusers*, by Francis P. Williamson, published by Flint & Company, in Philadelphia, in 1874; *Wickedness in High Places*, by Edmund B. Fairfield, published by Myers & Brothers, in Mansfield, Ohio, in 1874; *A Biography of the Rev. Henry Ward Beecher*, by William C. Beecher and S. Scoville, published by C. L. Webster & Co., in New York, in 1888; *Sunshine and Shadow*, by Matthew Hale Smith, published by J. B. Burr & Company, in Hartford, Conn., in 1869; *Incredible New York*, by Lloyd Morris, published by Random House, in New York, in 1951; the files or pamphlet summations of various newspaper accounts relating to the scandal and the trial, especially those of the *New York Times*; the pamphlets of Victoria Woodhull and the files of *Woodhull and Claflin's Weekly*; and the printed sermons of Henry Ward Beecher, taken from various sources. The pictures came from *Leslie's Illustrated Weekly*, from *Puck's* and from *Harper's Weekly*. The author wishes to thank, among others, particularly William Shawn, editor of the *New Yorker*, for having enabled him first to undertake this project, and Harold Strauss, editor-in-chief of Alfred A. Knopf, Inc., for his constant editorial advice.

Robert Shaplen
New York, 1954

CONTENTS

FREE LOVE

PART 1

NESTING ON THE HEIGHTS

CHAPTER I

On the night of July 3, 1870, Elizabeth Richards Tilton, a small, dark-haired woman of thirty-five, the mother of four children, confessed to her husband, Theodore, that she had committed adultery with her pastor, the Reverend Henry Ward Beecher, who was then the foremost preacher in the land. The evening was a sultry one, and Mrs. Tilton, who had been recuperating in the country from an illness, had returned unexpectedly at nine o'clock to her home, at 174 Livingston Street, on Brooklyn Heights, for the sole purpose of unburdening herself. She told Mr. Tilton, with what he later described as great modesty and delicacy, that her relations with Mr. Beecher had begun in the fall of 1868 when she had gone to him in search of consolation for the death of a young son. Having revered and loved her minister for many years, she had yielded to him in recompense, she said, for the sympathy he gave her in bereavement. Their intimacy had lasted a year and a half, until that spring. In admonishing her to guard their secret, Mr. Beecher had persuaded her to call it "nest-hiding," a romantic term he had coined as an intrepid nature-lover while watching birds build and protect their nests. He had repeatedly assured her that he shared a divine and valid love with her, and that their full expression of it was as proper as a handshake or a kiss.

Mrs. Tilton, who was a highly devout person, told her husband that though she had come to regret "the necessary deceit of concealment," she had felt justified before God in what she had done on Mr. Beecher's authority as "a great and holy man" that it was not sinful, that, in fact, God would not have permitted it had it been wrong.

The accumulated pressure of conscience that drove Elizabeth Tilton to confess her clandestine act was to lead to the greatest scandal of the era, culminating in two church councils and a sensational, if inconclusive, public trial that rocked the country. Beecher was a powerful symbol of the times, and the charge that threatened to blast him from his pulpit and blacken his famous family name was one with which the subconscious, if not the conscious, mind of the nation was passionately to identify itself, either to prove or disprove. Scarcely a man or a woman in America would not have an opinion about the pastor's innocence or guilt.

The ramifications of the Beecher-Tilton case were to fill the newspapers from coast to coast for months on end, and while its entertainment value was high, it ultimately was to cut such a wide swath through the vast area of contemporary debate over private versus public conduct, the function of the evangelical church, and the place of women in the expanding social scene, that its importance would transcend the titillation it caused. The pleas of Beecher's lawyers, that a victory for him would be "a verdict of safety and honor for everybody," preserving "the civilization and purity of American life," bespoke the emotional sentimentality of millions whose faith in the unmitigated contentment of the Victorian age was firm. Others, representing a new restlessness and skepticism, were less willing to accept the prescription. Their views would be expressed by bold, provocative journalists like Charles Dana of the *New York Sun*, bluntly proclaiming that Henry Ward Beecher was "an adulterer, a perjurer and a fraud," and that "his great genius and his Christian pretenses only make his sins the more horrible and revolting." Even when faced by all the evidence, notably Beecher's and Mrs. Tilton's self-inculpating letters, many Americans, especially women, could never believe the preacher had sinned. To believe it would not only demolish a hero but would destroy the foundations of their own elaborate morality.

The great passion play unfolded slowly. In spite of the sensation it was to create, the immediate results of Elizabeth Tilton's nocturnal confession to her husband were surprisingly unsensational. Perhaps because Tilton had suspected for some time that his wife's affection for her pastor was more than platonic, and because she was aware of his suspicion, Elizabeth extracted a promise from Theodore, as she spoke with measured grief of her pious adultery, that he would not harm Mr. Beecher. The Tiltons had been married by Beecher in 1855 in his ultra-fashionable Plymouth Church, the most successful church in America, and he had been an intimate of their household for a number of years before his more particular intimacy with its mistress had begun. He and Tilton had been the closest of friends, associated on the *Independent*, the best-known religious publication in the country, and in the anti-slavery fight and

ELIZABETH RICHARDS TILTON

other liberal causes. Tilton, in effect, had risen from Beecher's protege to partner, and while their views on occasion had differed, Tilton had regarded the minister as "my man of all men" and had "loved that man as well as I ever loved a woman." After thinking over carefully in the light of the past what his wife had told him, and after consulting the Gospel according to St. John, he resolved to condone if he could what she said she had done and to try to restore "her wounded spirit."

The following day, the Fourth of July, was celebrated by Henry Ward Beecher in Woodstock, Connecticut, at the summer home of Henry C. Bowen, a former dry-goods merchant who had lost one fortune in the period between the panic of 1857 and the start of the Civil War but had made another one as a publisher and printer. As the owner of the *Independent* and also of a daily newspaper, the *Brooklyn Union*, Bowen had again become one of the wealthiest men in Brooklyn. The two persons who had helped him most were Beecher and Tilton, the

THEODORE TILTON

first with his magic name and the second through his exceptional abilities as an editor. The lives of the three were strangely intertwined; they had been called, as a matter of fact, "The Trinity of Plymouth Church." It was Bowen who, in 1847, had been chiefly responsible for bringing Beecher to the church from his previous pastorate in Indianapolis. It was Beecher who had paved the way for Tilton's editorial success by helping him get a job as a general assistant on the *Independent*. It had been Tilton's idea to increase circulation by spreading Beecher's name, and a series of weekly contributions by the preacher, known as "The Star Papers," in time became the journal's best known feature.

In 1861, with his business fortunes at low ebb, Bowen had conceived the idea of combining what he considered to be his two chief assets. He had made Henry Ward Beecher, under obligation to him for the prominence he had helped the preacher attain, the editor of the *Independent*. Tilton was then managing editor. The arrangement had satisfied each member of "the trinity": Tilton retained full freedom in running the paper; Beecher's fame was carried even farther across the land; and Bowen's profits soared. But in 1862, just as Beecher, who had not always waxed so passionate on the subject, was bitterly decrying slavery and chastising Abraham Lincoln for letting the war languish and for delaying an emancipation proclamation, the preacher's polemical props were knocked out from under him, temporarily at least. Henry Bowen's popular and attractive wife, Lucy Maria, the mother of ten children, lay on her deathbed, at thirty-eight. One of the last things she whispered to her sallow, sunken-eyed husband, leaning over her with his flowing beard, was a terrible confession. It was exactly like the one Lib Tilton was to make to her husband in the summer of 1870.

Like Tilton, Bowen at first resolved to remain silent; Beecher even preached at the funeral of Lucy Bowen, who had not been the first and would not be the last to develop a passion for her pastor. But his column suddenly disappeared from the *Independent*, and he soon left in a hurry for England to stir up enthusiasm for the cause of the North. Tilton became the

Independent's editor. When Beecher returned, Bowen continued to occupy the most expensive pew in the church he regarded as his own creation, where each Sunday he listened to the man whose evangelical oratory had become a national tradition. After a time, however, Henry Bowen's rankling secret became too much for him, and he alluded to it in conversations with one or two friends, including Theodore Tilton, in a talk they had one day along the rail of the Fulton Ferry. Bowen, moreover, claimed he knew other secrets of Beecher's emotional life, and in one of his fitful moods he even wrote a letter to Tilton, in 1863, in which he said:

> I sometimes feel that I must break this silence, that I must no longer suffer as a dumb man, and be made to bear a load of grief most unjustly. One word from me would make a revolution through Christendom . . . You have just a little of the evidence from the great volume in my possession . . . I am not pursuing a phantom, but solemnly brooding over an awful reality.

By tacit consent, Bowen and Beecher never discussed the past with each other. For a long time Bowen had refused to set foot in Beecher's house, and the preacher's contributions to the *Independent* had been confined to advertising testimonials for sewing machines, pianos, and even for a truss—business was always business with Bowen. But as the coolness between the two men had become more marked, mutual friends in Plymouth Church, for the welfare of the community, had brought them together early in 1870. Kneeling on a chair, with a hand on Bowen's bony knee and tears streaming down his face, Beecher had declared: "Bowen, we must be friends," and had said that an open break between them would kill him. The two men had agreed to bury the past for good and to patch up their business differences; Beecher's sermons were to appear again in Bowen's weekly. Afterward they had walked, misty-eyed, through the streets together, sharing old memories. But almost immediately Bowen had resumed whispering that he

HENRY BOWEN

could drive Beecher out of Brooklyn. That he still hesitated even after Beecher had become editor of a rival religious weekly, the *Christian Union*, which began to take circulation away from the *Independent*, was due chiefly to the fact that the pastor's great reputation was of material concern to the rich new aristocracy of Brooklyn Heights, whose tax-free bonds supported Plymouth Church and helped raise real-estate values in the fledgling city, and whose collective morality and communal well-being were firmly founded on Beecher's warm Gospel of Love. If Bowen had refrained because of pride and for selfish reasons from accusing Beecher, he also represented the troubled conscience of those many Americans who felt that where scandal threatened it could better be swallowed by circumstance as well as by pomp.

So it was not strange that on the Fourth of July, 1870, at Woodstock, after President Grant's special train had arrived, Beecher delivered an impassioned patriotic speech, and then joined Henry Bowen in a friendly footrace on Woodstock Common. They finished last, puffing and laughing, with their arms around each other. It was the closest they had been in years, and Beecher reveled in the gay security of the moment. He knew nothing, and was not to learn for some time, of what little Lib Tilton had been telling her husband during the long night back on Livingston Street in Brooklyn. Nor could he foresee the vast and variegated anguish that was to gather in the breasts of both Tiltons and himself, and, after an agony of suspense and a lengthy conspiracy to suppress it, would burst over all their heads, to the mixed dismay and delight of the rest of the nation.

The nation was already caught between gaping and gasping at the growing cosmopolitan wickedness. On the other side of the river in New York, brought suddenly, if still only figuratively, closer by the start of construction on the Brooklyn Bridge (it was not to be opened until 1883), the conflict between the old respectability and the new laissez-faire attitudes toward behavior, both public and private, had been steadily mounting. The scandal arising out of the peculations of the flamboyant Jim Fisk and his partner, Jay Gould, would be crudely climaxed by Fisk's hotel-stairs murder in a quarrel over the beautiful but fickle Josie Mansfield. The relations between Gould and Fisk, who, Beecher thundered, was "abominable in his lusts," and William Marcy ("Boss") Tweed's political ring would stun the country when Tweed's downfall, heralded by the slashing cartoons of Thomas Nast and the attacks of the *New York Times*, would abruptly begin in the fall of 1871. That would be the main event, but ever since the end of the Civil War the moral standards of the metropolis had been decreasing with such appalling swiftness that New York was called a shining cesspool or a moneyed dragon writhing in its own "beglittered slime."

Money was certainly at the bottom of it all. The astonishing success of the new aristocrats of wealth, the men like Fisk who "got things done," created shocked but respectful admiration on the part of a good many Americans who read or heard about him, as well as mixed contempt and fear in the sedate homes of the genteel folk who stood by and watched while their more modest fortunes languished. Fisk and the men like him lent a new meaning to progress. The rapid turnover of immense fresh wealth saw families move from back-street shanties to Murray Hill brownstones in a matter of weeks. One of the best-known journalists of the day, Matthew Hale Smith, wrote that "the leaders of upper New York were, a few years ago, porters, stable-boys, coal-heavers, pickers of rags, scrubbers of floors, and laundry women. Coarse, rude, ignorant, uncivil and immoral many of them are still. They carry with them their vulgar habits, and disgust those who from social position are compelled to invite them to their houses."

The new users of money applied it to new uses, chiefly to the pursuit of pleasure. The city, in all respects, had become a contrast of lights and darks, of what Smith called "sunshine and shadow." Loud, lavish dance halls and gambling houses, open all the hours of the day and night, had sprung up alongside established homes, where the principal events of the week were still musicales, regular church attendance, and Sunday rides in Central Park in satined victorias. Inevitably, crime, corruption, and vice came in the wake of the war and wild pleasure-seeking. Petty swindling by panel thievery and other tricks matched the large-scale swindling that went on in Wall Street and in City Hall. The art of blackmail was refined and commonly practiced on gullible or overextended persons, especially on rich social scions and on out-of-town strangers, but also on unwitting preachers lured on ostensible missions of mercy to houses of assignation. There were nearly a thousand such establishments, and clergymen claimed there were twenty thousand prostitutes in the city. The police said there were only three thousand, but admitted it was impossible to estimate the number of street-walkers and "miscellaneous girls" who worked as part-time waitresses and barmaids.

As the Beecher-Tilton case was clearly to dramatize, there was a narrow line in the minds of most Americans between what constituted "vile women" and visionary reformers who seized upon the expansiveness of the times to demand more freedom in general for women. The vulgar love of pleasure and a passion for reform went hand in hand, it was widely thought, the one working wickedly upon the other. Even when it would be admitted by some that Elizabeth Tilton might have sinned, tortuous rationalization would suggest that she had fallen because she had allowed herself to be surrounded not so much by the arms of her pastor as by her husband's radical friends, with their everlasting talk about feminism and free love. The making of money might not be stopped, but the making of love still might, it was felt, or at least the public discussion and the flagrant display of it. Even before the war the demands of Susan B. Anthony and Elizabeth Cady Stanton for more liberal divorce laws and for the right of women successful in business to propose to men had shocked New Yorkers as much as had the matrimonial confusion in the lives of such brazen beauties as Lola Montez, the dancer, and Ada Clare, the literary "Queen of Bohemia," whose poems and passions were equally unrestrained and unprivate. After the war, when suggestive musical comedies and burlesque came along, it seemed only the natural order of events that Jim Fisk should move in and corner the new market in entertainment and pulchritude as

MRS. ELIZABETH CADY STANTON AND SUSAN B. ANTHONY

well as the old market in rails and stocks. Fisk had lately bought the Grand Opera House and became the producer of imported *opéra bouffe*, flaunting its risqué improprieties in the faces of respectable folk by accompanying its chic French stars around town. In the basement of the opera house he secreted a printing press, where, with the approval of Tweed and his henchmen, Fisk and Gould casually over-capitalized the Erie Railroad by fifty million dollars in one calendar year. Here was the perfect manifestation of the new wealth and the new hedonism brought conveniently together in a single, glittering setting.

The city was growing so fast in all respects that it was difficult to keep up with its changing patterns, geographical as well as genealogical. In the space of a few years, the center of Manhattan life had begun to shift violently uptown, catapulted by the new elevated lines that reached up to Central Park and then to the Harlem River. Washington Square, lower Fifth Avenue, and Murray Hill were still the fashionable areas, but hotels and apartment houses were being built farther up in the forties and fifties, and sharp real-estate men were already eying the Bronx.

In contrast to the bustle of New York, life in Brooklyn was still orderly and simple, though Brooklyn, too, was increasing rapidly in size. From orchards and cow pastures and a population in 1806 of fourteen hundred, nearly half colored, it had grown to a hundred thousand residents by 1850, three years after Henry Ward Beecher and his family moved there from the West. Back in 1825, on the same site where Henry Bowen and his friends were to erect Plymouth Church, the Presbyterian Church had been built near the shore on rough and open farmland owned by the propertied Hicks brothers, "Milk" and "Spitter" (so called because the first had run a milk route and the second could hit a stove at twenty-five feet with a spray of tobacco juice). From the swampy triangle of the Gowanus, the Wall about and the Ferry districts, the city had since reached out toward Atlantic Avenue, Court and Fulton streets. Much farther out, Coney Island was now coming into its own as a fashionable, and not so fashionable, resort. Brooklyn itself, however, even by 1870, had little to offer for entertainment. Backyard cockfight arenas had been supplanted by a few clubs, but most families led quiet, secluded lives and went to bed early except when there were church gatherings. On Saturdays, parents might take their children to lunch at Dent's, across Fulton Street, where mutton imported from England was featured. On special occasions a carriage might be hired for a trip across the river on the ferry to Dorian's or Delmonico's, famous for their North River shad, or to Booth's Theatre on Twenty-Third Street. The ferries were the first centers of social life, and one usually caught the same boat twice a day if one went to business in New York. From seven to nine in the morning and from five to seven in the afternoon, the fare was a penny; the rest of the time it was two cents.

The fashionable center of Brooklyn was the Heights, along the river. When Beecher had first arrived, the area was just beginning to be settled. Pigs still wandered around, and a regulation had been posted that "No bull is permitted to roam through the streets under fine of $500." The bulls, someone said, were all heading for Wall Street. Children had crossed Fulton Street to go to school, and there had been a sign near the church that told where they should be deposited when lost. Andrew Oakes; who ran a general store, had doubled as coroner and advertised "a splendid assortment of ready made mahogany, cherry and bilsted coffins, shrouds, caps, scarves and other appendages for funerals. Hearses always ready." It had perhaps been an exaggeration of the tone in Brooklyn, but in comparison to the beginning high-jinks across the East River it had been apt. It was a fact that Brooklyn folks were proud and self-sufficient and had always regarded themselves as happily aloof from the scandalous doings in Manhattan.

By the end of the Civil War, some of the finest homes in the East had appeared on the Heights and in its vicinity. The fanciest one belonged to Henry Bowen. It was a spacious Colonial mansion that covered half a block off Willow Street, was fronted by a colonnade of six columns, and was full of shining mirrors and chandeliers, fancy frescoes, stuffed Audubon birds, Aubusson carpets, and unopened books. Family portraits were carved into the furniture. The Bowens were among the few Brooklynites who entertained lavishly, serving their European guests terrapin and champagne.

After the Wall Street ferry, running across to the tip of Manhattan, was opened, a growing number of wealthy bankers, brokers and merchants came to live on the Heights instead of following the uptown drift in Manhattan. Old-time Brooklynites commented snobbishly that "intimate social life has now been submerged by the influx of alien influences and will never again be in evidence, but its memory will ever linger like the fragrance of an old-fashioned garden." Henry Ward Beecher, a relative newcomer himself, had been among the first to approve. One of the chief considerations of the new arrivals was a place to worship, and what they heard about Plymouth Church and the free-wheeling doctrine of its pastor surely helped attract them.

CHAPTER II

In the summer of 1870, at fifty-seven, Beecher was at the height of his career. He was earning $20,000 a year as pastor of Plymouth Church and another fifteen thousand lecturing and writing, far more than any other preacher in the country. Everything about Plymouth Church was big. Its congregation of two thousand was the largest in America; it boasted the largest and most expensive church organ, and paid its organist and sexton, as well as its minister, the largest salaries. In the twenty-three years since Henry Bowen had helped finance his transfer to Brooklyn from the West, after writing him thirty letters of persuasion, Beecher had succeeded admirably in his declared aim of developing "that social, contagious spirit which we call a revival of religion." The books the trustees kept attested to this: the annual income from pew rentals had gone up from $10,000 to $60,000 over two decades, while the amount taken in from collections had risen from a few thousand to $40,000 a year. There was no doubt that Plymouth Church was big business. Its Sunday school room, complete with fountain, flowers, melodeon and piano as well as baby organ, and its social parlors and lecture room, were no longer ridiculed, as they had been at first, by other churches in America; if the others could afford them, they were copied.

On Sunday mornings, Orange and Cranberry streets outside "Beecher's Theater," as the church was called, were packed with visitors who had come across the river on the early-morning ferries nicknamed "Beecher Boats." The bustle was like that created by the arrival of a circus in a country town. The comparison was apt, for the crowds came as much to see Beecher perform as to hear him preach. At ten twenty, after all the regular pew-holders were seated, the police guarding the double line of people in the street were given the signal. Non-members were then allowed to fill the remainder of the 2,100 seats that ran in semicircular rows of lush upholstered red around the white and pink-tinged interior. After all the seats were taken, several hundred chairs and stools were put in the aisles and along the walls. Throughout the two-hour service, the vestibules remained jammed with standees.

The pulpit was of olive wood from the garden of Gethsemane, but Beecher seldom used it. As the organ played,

CROWDS OUTSIDE PLYMOUTH CHURCH

he stepped out quietly from a small door in the rear, a black leather hymn book in one hand and his familiar black hat in the other. He threw the hat upon the flower-decked platform and sat down in a simple armchair next to it. The platform, more than the pulpit, gave him room to display his dramatic talent, which matched his flamboyant vocabulary. He could, and invariably did, make his audiences laugh and cry, playing on the whole gamut of emotions. He was full of anecdotes and acted out complete scenes with grotesque facial contortions, stamping his foot, thumping his fists, chasing his antagonist up and down the platform as the sweat stood out on his brow and his cheeks glowed. Frequently he himself wept in unabashed empathy as he played such roles as a drunken man before a judge. He would pretend to be a blacksmith at a forge, a back-woodsman chopping a tree. Once he imitated a fisherman catching a trout. He threw the fly, hooked a fish, dodged up and down as he reeled in, and finally landed his imaginary quarry. It was all so vivid that a man in front stood up and shouted: "By God, he's got him!" Beecher always favored this dramatic approach, and his figures were often drawn from nature and experience. When one of his violent contests was over, he would pause, mop his face, let a broad smile suffuse it, and in tones as gentle as a woman's conduct a prayer. Hearty, colloquial, vehement, and dogmatic, he was also tender, soft, and rever-ent, and when he spoke the Word of God he made it sound as if Jesus were speaking through him in a personal vein. It was said that those who listened to him, entranced, "were like the pipes and stops of a great organ, while he was the master who played upon them."

Beecher kept closely in touch with the affairs of the nation and, both in his sermons and in his Friday-evening lectures, as well as in his public lecturing and in what he wrote, he took an active stand on the burning issues of the day. Despite his degree of tardiness in adopting a firm moral and social position against slavery and then holding it, there was little doubt that he had eventually played an important emotional role in the fight to free the Negroes. On two occasions he had followed his Sunday sermon by raising money in church to deliver pretty young slave girls from bondage. The scenes had been hysterical. The slaves stood on the platform alongside him as women in the congregation cried and tore off their bracelets and men unfastened their watches and threw them into the collection baskets. "Sabbath harlequinades—motley in the pulpit," *Vanity Fair* later called his performances.

Of medium height, with broad shoulders and a chest that made him seem powerful despite a growing corpulence, Beecher had a ruddy, moon-shaped face, surmounted by a high, wide brow. His large gray eyes were expressively slanted. His nose was fleshly, and he had a prominent, full mouth. His graying hair hung boldly down, reaching the edge of his long black jacket. He was not handsome, but beyond the heartiness and geniality was a magnetic quality that almost everyone who met him, out of the church as well as in, responded to fervidly. "The men admire him, the women adore him, and the children all love him," a biographer wrote. There was a captivating, unministerial quality to his pursuit of creature comforts, and "nothing in his appearance," a friend observed, "is indicative of days of fasting or nights of prayer." A man of impulse and sudden inspiration, he would compose his sermons an hour before delivering them, to retain the full excitement of creation. "Some men like their bread cold, some like it hot," he said. "I like mine hot." He once said that he extended himself in bad weather so that his audience would be sure to turn out. "It snowed and rained nearly every Sabbath in a certain winter," he explained, "and the effort I had to make to remain faithful to this rule came near killing me."

Beecher opposed all didactic creeds—they were "husks that conceal the corn"—and preached a variety of doctrine that would sound Calvinist one week and Universalist the next. His church was Congregationalist, and Beecher took full advantage of the latitude this denomination allowed him. "What is Orthodoxy?" he asked. "I will tell you. Orthodoxy is *my* doxy, and Heterodoxy is *your* doxy, that is if your doxy is not like *my* doxy." Neither his dress nor his manner was that of other ministers; he wore no clerical collar and had his broad-brim, soft-felt hats made to order. He preferred square-toed, Puritan-father shoes. "Did I, when I became a minister, cease to be a man or a citizen?" he inquired. "No! A thousand times no! Have I not as much interest in our government as though I were a lawyer, a ditchdigger or a wood-sawyer? Out upon this idea that a minister must *dress* minister, *walk* minister, *talk* minister, *eat* minister and wear his ministerial badge as a convict wears his stripes."

Beecher inherited his revivalist doctrine from his Presbyterian father, Lyman Beecher, who had fought the anti-Christ on Long Island, in Connecticut, in Boston, and finally in Cincinnati, where he had been accused and acquitted of heresy because he had sought to temper the old, harsh doctrine of his mother church in his private Congregational furnace. Lyman, like his son, was also at his best when roused to fever pitch. He used to keep a load of sand in his cellar to throw about when he was tense, and in his back yard he had parallel bars and other gymnastic equipment. After he had preached, he would return home and relax by playing the violin or danc-ing "the double shuffle," an old New England barn jig, for his seven sons, all of whom followed him into the ministry, and his four daughters.

Henry Ward, who as a child had no toys, a fact that engen-dered his ostentatious love of jewels in later life—he always carried uncut opals, which he called undying flowers, in his pockets—had been a failure at school until he lost his stam-mer and halting ways and paraded in a white suit and a black cap with the band at Amherst. He had begun as a rural pastor in Lawrenceburg, Indiana, where he had swept the church out, built the fires, ridden itinerantly, and preached violently to a tiny congregation against drunkenness and the devil. In Indianapolis he had continued his battle against vice. Dressing in casual Western style, he had described himself as "a lub-berly fellow," but he had already begun to acquire that peculiar appeal to women which, when he came East, brought him a hundred lovesick letters a day. A young girl who had lived next

BEECHER PREACHING IN PLYMOUTH CHURCH

door remembered him years later as "a great, good-natured, talented, romping booby of a boy." She recalled "many a romp on summer evenings" when "girls and preacher rushed pell-mell after each other around the parsonage, and Mr. Beecher stationed himself at the rain barrel and, using his straw hat for a dipper, baptized the girls thoroughly, though quite independently, of the ceremonies of the church." Another of the girls, Betty Bates, the fourteen-year-old daughter of a prominent Indiana family, had unabashedly worshipped and then fallen madly in love with the young minister. She never married, and it was always a little hazy how thoroughly Beecher, notwithstanding his advice to young men to run from temptation, had reciprocated her affections. He had been married, at the age of twenty-four, to Eunice Bullard, the prim daughter of a New England Puritan family, and whether it was really that his wife's health was failing in the West, the reason he ascribed, or that there was more than met the eye in Miss Bates, he suddenly accepted Henry Bowen's summons. At thirty-four, he moved to Brooklyn, bringing with him Eunice and their three children. Six more children were to be born in the East.

For the first few weeks the Beechers had stayed with the Bowens, but then they had moved into a three-story brownstone on Columbia Heights, three blocks from the church. There was an old-fashioned parlor downstairs, with walls divided into panels and a wooden ledge that ran around the room four feet off the floor. The furniture was a chaos of styles. Ornaments of bronze and plaster abounded among autumn leaves. Looking out on the bay in back was Beecher's study, with a large, flat-top desk in the center. Engravings and portraits were hung all around. There were a fireplace with a small grill, and several high-backed chairs.

Beecher began his day at six, often seeing out-of-town visitors before breakfast, which consisted usually of a Spanish mackerel and coffee. He would write and read all morning, and in the afternoon, from two to four, would see more visitors. Strangers and intimates alike received the full benefit of his expansive sympathy, what he called "love without stint." There were always half a dozen or more waiting, and from time to time he would emerge from the study like a doctor to usher the next one in with a hearty "How are you, old fellow?"

Eunice Beecher ran not only the house but also the mundane affairs of her husband's life, so that he could minister freely. A combined partner and mother to him, she took care of his finances and opened and answered his mail. A forbearing, humorless woman whom Brooklynites secretly called "The Griffin," she was scarcely the perfect mate for his exuberant, outpouring soul. She was both jealous and contemptuous of the emotional response which he seemed so easily to evoke in other women, and which he did not always hold back in return. One Sunday after his attachment to Lucy Bowen had begun, with a boldness and a baring of his own inner self that was typical of him, Beecher preached on the subject of marriage. "Domestic unhappiness comes from the fact that people do not enough recognize the peculiarities of each other's natures," he said, and he spoke of "a flaming, demonstrative nature" having to deal with "a cool, undemonstrative" one. There was little doubt that, in spite of all his activities, the pastor was a lonely man.

Among those who came to Plymouth Church while still a young boy, to whom Beecher was later to confide his loneliness and whose frequent young companion, Elizabeth Richards, was to consider it her bounden duty to assuage him, was Theodore Tilton. A shoemaker's son who stemmed from an old West England family, Tilton was born in New York in 1835. After being graduated from the Free Academy, the precursor of the College of the City of New York, where a friend had described him as "having an intensity both at work and play that was frightful," he went to work as a reporter on Horace Greeley's *New York Tribune*. Then he switched to the *New York Observer*, where he became an expert in shorthand, or phonography, as it was then called. A tall and extremely handsome young man, with Grecian features, soft, expressive eyes, and plentiful auburn hair, which he wore long and curled in back, he was described by an associate as "a perfect Adonis, with whom any woman of sentiment and refinement would fall in love."

Attracted by Beecher's boyish charm, Tilton grew so to admire the sermons of the preacher that he took them down verbatim. Beecher in turn found Tilton of "an engaging manner and comely appearance," and with his ready sense of publicity was not at all averse to the young man's self-dedication as an enthusiastic amanuensis.

As for Elizabeth Richards, the serious, sentimental, and religious-minded sister of a school friend of Tilton's, Joseph Richards, she weighed scarcely a hundred pounds and was not beautiful, but she also had lovely dark eyes that matched her dark hair, which she wore in ringlets, and a small face that glowed quite handsomely when she was aroused, as she invariably was when she listened to Henry Ward Beecher. Beecher had known her since she was ten, at first as belonging to a set of girls attending school with his daughter and church with her family. She introduced Tilton to the church, and when they were wed there Beecher remembered them as "one of the fairest pairs that I ever married." The ceremony was "a beautiful picture," he said, adding that "I had very strong sympathies for their future."

It was in the following spring of 1856 that, on Beecher's suggestion, Bowen offered young Tilton a job as assistant on the *Independent.* The influence of the religious or family paper, striking out against all forms of vice and corruption and bad manners, was still considerable, but the *Independent*'s circulation was lagging at seventeen thousand. Tilton, who had just refused another job on a daily paper because he would not work on Sundays, was held to be one of the promising journalists in New York, and he soon proved his worth to Bowen. The weekly had suffered, in part, by adopting an advanced position in the fight against slavery, criticizing, for example, the powerful Tract Society. Without changing its stand, and, as a matter of fact, stepping up the Abolitionist campaign, Tilton widened the scope of the *Independent.* Contributions debating all the important social and political questions of the day, from a secular as well as a moral and religious point of view, were obtained from such eminent men as Wendell Phillips, James

A HAPPIER PASTORAL MOMENT

Tilton and his wife vacationing in upstate New York.

Russell Lowell, Bayard Taylor, William M. Evarts, William Lloyd Garrison, Greeley, and others. From abroad came poems by Elizabeth Barrett Browning and political comment from the Hungarian patriot Louis Kossuth. Tilton attracted great attention to himself by successfully debating a slavery issue with his idol, Beecher, who was not yet in a final uncompromising anti-slavery mood. The young man became a recognized orator with a dashing platform style, a professional lecturer in his own right, and his powerful editorials in the weekly on a variety of subjects, including women's rights, put it in the forefront of liberal reform drives. He wrote poetry too, chiefly love poems and poems for children. The *Independent* soon paid off its original indebtedness in full. Its circulation reached sixty thousand, and it became the most profitable religious journal in the world, and the best-paying paper in America except for the *New York Herald*. Tilton's own salary increases reflected the paper's success. He began in 1856 at $700 a year. After becoming editor, he got $7,000, and he later received a contract for a total of $15,000 as a profit-sharing contributor to the weekly and the editor of Henry Bowen's daily paper, the *Brooklyn Union*. These were large figures, especially for those days, and Tilton's fortune grew ample in other respects as well. He owned a share of the *Tribune* worth $10,000, bought a small farm in Iowa, and valued his house and possessions in Brooklyn at $25,000.

Almost from the very beginning of their relationship, Tilton and Beecher had been inseparable. The younger man's unquenchable idealism and romanticism stimulated Beecher and appealed to his hunger for emotional release. Every Wednesday, after reading the first proofs of the *Independent*, the two men took off for Manhattan, where they ambled for hours among the bookshops and the picture galleries. "It was common employments, companionship and downright loving on my part," Beecher said. The preacher was "the most charming man I ever saw" to Tilton. "What hours we had together!" he later wrote. "What mutual revelations and communings! What interchanges of mirth, of tears, of prayers!" Two years after Beecher had mailed him a letter full of affection from England,

and despite the first political differences they had come to have, Tilton penned a midnight declaration to his pastor:

> My friend, from my boyhood up you have been to me what no other man has been, what no other man can be . . . The intimacy with which you have honored me for twelve years has been, next to my wife and family, the chief affection of my life . . . You are my minister, teacher, father, brother, friend, companion. The debt I owe you I can never pay . . . Whether you have been high or low, great or common, I believe that my heart, knowing its mate, would have loved you exactly the same . . . Our friendship is yet of this earth, earthy; but it shall one day stand uplifted above mortality, safe, without scar or law, without a breath to blot or a suspicion to endanger it.

He signed it "your unworthy but eternal friend." It was a fair example of the breast-heaving literary style of the day.

One thing marred the friendship. Eunice Beecher hated Tilton. She knew that it was he who had influenced her husband to support liberal causes she thought he had no business to deal with. When Tilton had taken it upon himself in 1861 to prevent a Beecher family scandal by securing a commission for a son who had got into a barroom brawl, Beecher had regarded it "exquisitely," but Eunice had been furious over the intervention. Thenceforth Tilton never entered the Beecher home when she was there, nor would she set foot in his house, where such ilk as Phillips, John G. Whittier, and Greeley were often overnight guests. The Tiltons, in fact, ran a considerable salon. Their home was rambling and comfortable, with a wide, five-columned porch, an elegant parlor, and winding staircases connecting the floors in rear and front. Across a wooden archway just beyond the entrance was a carved inscription: "And into whatsoever house ye enter, ye shall first say, 'Peace be to this house.'" Devotional art attested plentifully to the bent of Lib Tilton's mind.

An editorialist was to comment that "The Tiltons were a poetic, gushing people who veiled everything with a thin mystery of glamour. Even their furniture had a garish glow." But Beecher loved the place. "O, Theodore, God might strip all other gifts from me if he would only give me a wife like Elizabeth and a home like yours," he once told Tilton. He made no bones about his romantic dissatisfaction at home and often spoke about the "hungry needs" of his heart. Tilton kept inviting him over, but the preacher came only irregularly at first, until Tilton scolded him for his "neglect," later putting it ruefully: "I thought I was stealing away too large a share of him and that my wife ought to have a larger part of him." As Mrs. Tilton was shy and could scarcely express her admiration for Beecher, Tilton took it upon himself to tell the pastor that "There is one little woman down at my house who loves you more than you have an idea of." So Beecher gave in and came more often.

THE TILTON HOUSE AT 174 LIVINGSTON STREET

When he returned from England in 1863, he brought Lib Tilton a Brazilian topaz brooch. It was "of little intrinsic value," just part "of that bric-a-brac folly that travelers who have never been abroad but once bring back home with them," he said, and when he gave it to her, Elizabeth burst out laughing, mistaking it at first for a pillbox she thought her husband had given him to bring her from downtown. But it was a beginning of attention. Because Tilton was out of town so much, lecturing from fall to spring, Beecher took to calling regularly. It was something Horace Greeley, much as he liked the Tiltons, refused to do. Even though he had lived in their home for a time, he told Theodore he did not think it proper to visit the wife of a friend who was away. But Beecher was a pastor, not especially a visiting one, he said, but one who went through "paroxysms of visitation"—paroxysms was one his favorite words—and since he had been importuned, he was always able to include Elizabeth Tilton in his rounds, whether Theodore was home or not. "During these years of intimacy in Mr. Tilton's family, I was treated as a father or elder brother," he was to explain. "Children were born, children died. They learned to love me, and to frolic with me as if I were one of themselves. I loved them and I had for Mrs. Tilton a true and honest regard. She seemed to me an affectionate mother, a devoted wife . . . turning to me with artless familiarity and with entire confidence. Childish in appearance, she was childlike in nature, and I would as soon have misconceived the confidence of her little girls as the unstudied affection she showed me."

CHAPTER III

When he used such words as "artless" and "childlike" to describe Lib Tilton, Henry Ward Beecher demonstrated one of the attributes of his character for which he was most admired, his keen knowledge of human nature. She was in many ways a child of his own cult, for the shielding sentimentality and emotionalism in her make-up, if he had not initially inspired it, had been surely nurtured in the atmosphere of Plymouth Church, in which more than one worshipping female had been led to closely identify love of pastor with love of God. It was a safe, hermetic little world.

Even as a girl, Lib Tilton had been affectionate and outgiving. As a student at Packer Institute, steeping herself in romantic novels and poetry, she had been described by her teachers as "a strangely earnest little brunette" whose "interesting" if not pretty face, the best feature of which was her probing eyes, had a pleasant way of lighting up when a subject excited her. As she grew older she had begun to devote herself to works of charity, and when she joined Plymouth Church she had become a leader of the bethel associated with it for helping the poor. She had taught in the Sunday school, too, and had been religiously strict from the start with her own children and had not permitted them to play with dolls on the Sabbath. Theodore Tilton was to echo the opinion of Beecher when he later called his wife, though he put it in the past, "sympathetic to a very rich degree" and "a very lovely woman who did good to whomsoever she touched."

When Beecher returned from England, there was another reason why Tilton had been able to persuade him to come more often to the house on Livingston Street. Without his old job and associations on the *Independent*, which Lucy Bowen's dying confession to her husband had put an end to, the preacher was lonelier than ever, even though he still had

THE EDUCATION OF THE LADIES
Beecher on the doorstep of his house,
explaining religious doctrine to female worshippers.

his church and his lecture platforms. Tilton's salon numbered not only well-known men of letters but also prominent Republicans and leaders of the women's movement, among them Miss Anthony, Mrs. Stanton, and Laura Curtis Bullard. Tilton had always said he wanted his wife "to share in anything that I had," and his friendship with the preacher was included. Beecher, in turn, obtained at the Tiltons' a fresh sense of participation he felt he needed. He also needed a new cause to be at his dramatic best in the pulpit. Women, whose adulation had always provided such a large part of his fashionable success and whose social status was soon to undergo a significant change, seemed an apt subject for his unbounding consideration and zeal.

One rainy afternoon, walking along Brooklyn Heights, he spotted Miss Anthony, tall and spare, walking ahead of him. Catching up with her, he clapped her vigorously on the back and asked: "Well, old girl, what do you want now?" Miss Anthony was on her way to attend a suffragist meeting at the Tiltons', and the question, which Beecher might have asked of himself, ironically projected the future. Henceforth, both in his private and in his pastoral life, the head of Plymouth Church was to be more active in behalf of women. While he was to end in the more moderate camp of Julia Ward Howe, he already held inner convictions about the freedom of personal relations, associated with the question of the emancipation of women, that were not only more liberal than those of Miss Anthony and her friends but seemed very like those to be loudly espoused by the most radical of all fighters for women's rights, Victoria Woodhull, the exponent of what was already called "free love." Mrs. Woodhull, to Beecher's intense embarrassment, was to claim him as one of her own and to demand that he preach what he practiced.

This was still some years off, but there was less and less doubt that the marriage contract, as far as Beecher was concerned, had by now left him emotionally shortchanged to the point of bankruptcy. The tales about the sad home life of the Beechers had become common gossip, and Beecher himself

MRS. BEECHER, "THE GRIFFIN"

helped spread them. He could not stand Eunice Beecher's cold disapproval of almost everything he did, her stern way of treating him and his foibles, the way she looked down upon his enthusiasms and his love of life. Their breakfast conversation, he had told Tilton, was "the vainest, the most vapid, the most juiceless, the most unsaccharine of all things." Life, to be good for Beecher, had presumably to be saccharine.

Mrs. Beecher's lack of sympathy for her husband had reached a point where she had virtually thrown his father, Lyman Beecher, and Lyman's third wife, out of the house, not long before the old man died and was accorded by his son a vast and panoramic funeral service at Plymouth Church. Eunice Beecher's fierce opposition to the marriage of Harriet Eliza Beecher, the first child she and Henry Ward had had back in Indiana, had made Beecher cry when he told Tilton about it. Life with his wife, Beecher said, had become "a hell on earth," and now, to make matters worse, Eunice was violently against the image of the new woman, as Susan Anthony and others envisioned her. Formally, Mrs. Beecher believed in "the sweeter, more delicate and feminine home duties" as firmly as she held to other rigid precepts from her past. It did not make things easier for Beecher that she was backed up by at least two vocal sisters of his, Catherine and Harriet Beecher Stowe, the author of *Uncle Tom's Cabin.*

In the strange unfolding of events there was a fateful irony. One thing led to another in such perfect concatenation that truth indeed became stranger than fiction, even as written by such ultra-romantics as Charles Reade and Mrs. E. D. E. N. Southworth, two of Elizabeth Tilton's favorites. Beecher's sense of deprivation; Lib Tilton's private romantic world, from which for her husband's sake she was trying to reach out, at least to the extent of welcoming his proselytizing guests to the house and identifying herself to a limited degree with Miss Anthony's campaign; and, finally, Tilton's tormented wrestlings with his conscience as he found his faith in God diminishing and as he came more and more to identify himself with causes opposed by the church—all added up to inevitable tragedy. His frequent absences from home simply provided the circumstantial framework.

Tilton had begun life as an extreme Calvinist. "I would have cut off my right hand rather than have written a letter on a Sabbath day," he explained. "I was brought up to the conviction that all men were miserable sinners." When he had met Elizabeth and they had become lovers—she had been only seventeen and he sixteen, and their passion had apparently overcome any scruples about pre-marital relations—she had wanted him to become a clergyman. Gradually, however, as he came under the influence of Unitarianism, Tilton found his religious views shifting more violently than his wife's. While not rejecting the divinity of Christ completely, Tilton came to regard skeptically the theory of Christ's deity and to question various other doctrines of the church, including the notion of Hell. Tilton was the first to admit that the change in his views "produced upon her mind a good deal of unhappiness," but when, after what he described as "four years of struggle and laceration" in his early thirties, he turned from the church with a vengeance as he became an Abolitionist, his conduct became all the more painful to his devout wife, who would not even receive guests on church days. In contrast, Tilton was ultimately seen "rolling balls" (playing billiards) on Sundays.

Into this picture stepped Henry Ward Beecher, who, Tilton would later say, in emphasizing that Elizabeth should indeed have married a minister, "took advantage of her orthodox views to make her the net and mesh in which he ensnared her," until "I think she regarded Mr. Beecher as though Jesus Christ himself had walked in" in a time of troubles. Constantly worried about her own soul, as well as her husband's, whose free-thinking ways seemed to be carrying him further and further from the home as well as the church, Elizabeth Tilton began confiding in her pastor. It was a natural enough thing to do. Beecher counseled patience. He, too, was worried about his protege's "loose doctrine of inspiration" and about Tilton's strange new belief in evolution and his advocacy of more liberal divorce, he said, but he told Elizabeth that Theodore was simply "in a transitional state." Modestly, he later explained that "her mind was seriously troubled as to her duty, and I attempted to enlighten her." He praised Elizabeth, in her unhappiness over her husband's apostasy, for her nobility and her unique combination of "ecstatic devotion, serenity, peace and trust in God." Then he sat down and wrote a long letter to Tilton, who was on the road lecturing, warning him, in her behalf, "not to accept things from poetic or emotive reasons which are but half-true."

The writing of letters and diaries in a day before the telephone was invented was the chief means of unburdening oneself, and Elizabeth, as her personal torment increased with the onset of temptation, likewise took quill in hand. She both kept a diary and wrote at length to her wandering husband. In an almost mystic sense, with what amounted to pre-carnal guilt, she tried to explain to him the nature of the vacuum in her life that Beecher was filling. It was as if she knew the dangers ahead but was seeking to deny them by rationalization. Late in

December 1866, addressing herself to "My Own True Mate," she wrote:

. . . My beloved, I have been thinking of my love for Mr. B. considerably of late, and those thoughts you shall have . . . Now, I think I have lived a richer, happier life since I have known him. And have you not loved me more ardently since you saw another high nature appreciated me? It is not possible for any human creature to supersede you in my heart . . . But to return to Mr. B. He has been the guide of our youth . . . During these early years, the mention of his name, to meet him, or better still, a visit from him, my cheek would flush with pleasure—an experience common to all his parishioners of both sexes. It is not strange, then, darling, that on a more intimate acquaintance my delight and pleasure should increase. Of course, I realize what attracts you both to me is a supposed purity of soul you find in me. Therefore it is that never before have I had such wrestlings with God, that He would reveal Himself to me . . . It is true that I live in an agony of soul daily; nevertheless, I am profoundly happy in my privileges, opportunities and blessings. . .

A month later:

. . . Mr. B. called Saturday. He came tired and gloomy, but he said I had the most calming and peaceful influence over him. I believe he loves you. We talked of you. He brought me two pretty flowers in pots, and said as he went out, 'What a pretty house this is.' . . . It would make me very happy if you could look in upon us without his knowing it.

The children are passing through the stage of the hooping [sic] cough very comfortably thanks to homeopathy. . .

Signing herself variously as "Wife," "Wifey," "Your Own Wife," and "Wife Elizabeth," Mrs. Tilton gave her husband a running account of the conflict that had come to plague her. Early in 1867 she wrote:

> Oh, how my soul yearns over you two dear men! I commit you both to God's love . . . Why I was so mysteriously brought in as an actor in this friendship, I know not, yet no experience of my whole life has made my soul ache so verily . . . I do love him dearly, and I do love you supremely, utterly, believe it. Perhaps, if by God's grace I keep myself white, I may bless you both. I am striving. God bless this trinity.

This sort of desperate effort to avoid taking the awful, irrevocable step that seemed more inevitable every day was spelled out by Elizabeth in letter after letter. The theme she constantly played upon was the figurative one of creating a cozy trinity instead of a catastrophic triangle.

A year later, not too long before her adultery began, she told Tilton:

> . . . I *know* that now mother, children or friend have no longer possession of my heart . . . About eleven o'clock today, Mr. B. called. Now, beloved, let not even the shadow of a *shadow* fall on your dear heart because of this, henceforth or forever. He cannot by *any possibility* be much to me, since I have known you . . . Do not think it audacious in me to say I am to him a good deal . . . You once told me you did not believe that I gave you a correct account of his visits, and you always felt that I repressed much. Sweet, do you still believe this? I strive in my poor word-painting to give you the *spirit* and impression which I gave to him, and he to me. It would be my supreme wish and delight to have you *always with me.* This trinity of friendship I pray for always.

As for Tilton, moving around from hotel to hotel, lecturing from New England to "the far west" of Iowa and Minnesota, beset by his own doubts, his wife's letters scarcely alleviated his inner tension. Traveling encouraged his loneliness and gloom, and he veered from habitual self-commiseration to occasional flashes of firm resolve to recapture the faith that seemed to be escaping from him. From Indiana, in 1866, he wrote:

> . . . I am not jealous . . . I think any man is a fool who is jealous . . . But I am somewhat disturbed and have been for a long while past at the diminishing faith which I entertain for human nature. Human characters do not seem to me as lovely as they once did . . . During my travels I have had profound reflections on my life. I am a weak man, supposed to be strong; a selfish man, supposed to be the world's lover and helper; an earthly minded man, supposed to be more Christian than my fellows. I cannot endure the mockery; it breeds agony in me. At this moment I am completely wretched . . . I feel myself scarred, spotted, miserable and unworthy . . . My life is so unprofitable that I sometimes dare not turn around and look upon it . . . My prayers of late have all seemed spiritless without you . . . If you should ever appear to me anything less than the ideal woman, the Christian saint that I know you to be, I shall not care to live a day longer . . .

A few days later, planning to meet Mrs. Tilton in the West, a trip that did not eventuate, Tilton wrote from Dubuque, Iowa, with mockery and self-pity:

> . . . I don't expect . . . to be lonesome much longer, for I am to meet you in Chicago. Now that the *other* man has gone off lecturing (as your letter mentions) you can afford to come see *me* . . . Leave home, children, kith and kin, and cleave unto him to whom you originally promised to cleave. You promised the *other* man to cleave to *me*, and

yet you leave *me all alone* and cleave to *him*. 'O Frailty! Thy name is woman!' If you can get anybody to pour tea for you, and to take sauce from the servants, and to receive pastoral visits, I shall expect to meet you . . .

Elizabeth remarked about his gathering moodiness. She noted: "You have six epistles ending: 'Yours in dust and ashes,' 'Yours doggedly,' 'God help your sorrowful and groaning husband,' 'Yours achingly,' etc." Addressing himself to her as "My Dear Orthodox Wife," Tilton wrote sadly that "the old religious teachings, the orthodox view, the dread of punishment, the atonement, have less and less power over my mind." In another letter, he wrote at length of his diminishing faith in the divinity of Christ, declaring that if history showed Christ to have been a married man, the fact would "humanize" him. He signed himself: "Your Heterodox Husband."

RECONCILED?
Beecher dances a jig over the Tiltons' efforts to patch up their marriage.

Elizabeth was caught in a wild whirl in which her love for the pastor and the mystic appeal of his church were mixed with her anguish over Theodore and with her sorrow for both men in their separate emotional voids. Her guilt grew more penultimately acute, and just before her battle of doubt gave way to decision, she and her husband outdid each other in a torrent of self-recrimination. Tilton saw himself "a hypocrite, a deceiver, 'a whited sepulchre filled with dead men's bones,'" and Elizabeth wrote back: "I am haunted by the remorse of knowing that, because of my harshness and indifference to you, you were driven to despair, perhaps sin . . . I am the chief of sinners!"

How wayward Tilton was or was not was never made certain, though Beecher's cohorts and defenders were to delve thoroughly into his past. They were to claim adulteries on his part to support their case, including what became known as "The Winsted Scandal." This unproved episode involving Tilton and the seventeen-year-old daughter of a Congressman, aptly named Lovejoy, was supposed to have taken place in Winsted, Connecticut, when the girl accompanied Tilton there on a lecture. Hotel employees said that they saw her and Tilton sitting together in front of a fire and that her dress was undone. Tilton denied it, vehemently. "*I* never saw her with her dress unbuttoned," he gallantly declared. There was supposed to be another girl, unnamed, out West, and Mrs. Tilton was to quote her husband as saying that if he felt of a mind, he would not hesitate to take a woman while on the road and lonely. There was little doubt that Tilton's "loose opinions about marriage," as Beecher described them, were exciting comment. The phrase "free love" was increasingly being bandied about, and while Tilton characterized it in an article he wrote as "a beautiful term designating a revolting thing," he was more and more in favor of liberalizing the divorce laws. In one of the endless open-letter exchanges of the day, he wrote to Horace Greeley that "I would no more permit the law of the land to enchain me to a woman whom I did not love, or who did not love me, than I would permit the same law to handcuff me as a slave to a master on a plantation." And he quoted John Milton to support his argument that "whatever nullifies marriage justifies divorce."

The Tiltons had living with them in 1868, in addition to their five children ranging from Florence, aged eleven, to babies Paul and Carroll, a fluctuating retinue of servants that sometimes numbered six; Mrs. Tilton's mother, Mrs. Nathan B. Morse; and a seventeen-year-old girl named Bessie Turner. Bessie had come to the Tiltons in 1864 from the West under the name of Lizzie McDermott, "a little waif of a thing," as Tilton described her. Mrs. Tilton had heard about her through a former Sunday school teacher and had brought her to Brooklyn as a servant-girl. On one of his trips Tilton later established that her real name was Turner. She stayed in the household for eight years and came to be regarded as a member of the family; in effect, though not formally, she was an adopted child. By the time she left she had grown into a handsome, self-possessed young woman whose account of Tilton's conduct in the house during the years of her residence was to be extremely damaging to him.

Bessie's descriptions of what went on in Livingston Street were as amusing as they were bitter. Where Mrs. Tilton had "a lovely and amiable disposition" and was always ready to serve every whim of her husband's, from offering him small, choice oysters at breakfast to his slippers at night, Tilton, according to Bessie, was "a very selfish man, very hard, very irritable, very fastidious, very dogmatical in his manner and unsociable in his disposition." For days at a time, Bessie related, he would make everyone in the house nervous and unhappy by stalking sullenly through the rooms and halls. On occasion he would loudly berate Mrs. Tilton in front of all the children for her alleged lack of economy or for serving him something he did not like, and at least twelve times he locked her up for three or four hours and lectured her about her shortcomings. He would emerge from these sessions with his face "red as fury," Bessie said, and Mrs. Tilton "would come out crying." When her husband was moody and bad-tempered, Mrs. Tilton "would kneel down beside the sofa and stroke his hair and do everything to make him feel happy," but Tilton would just get more impatient with her. In front of guests he complained about her grammar, and embarrassed her by disparaging her tininess, saying such things as "Elizabeth, stand to one side—don't keep near me, I don't wish any comparisons drawn, the contrast is too great," and "I would give $500 if you were not by my side." Mrs. Tilton herself once said: "I would have cut off my right arm to be five inches taller."

Tilton's idiosyncrasies, said Bessie, included a habit of wandering through the house in his nightclothes, taking pictures from the walls and re-hanging them in different places. This went on sometimes after midnight, she said, and she remembered one night specifically when she had been unable to sleep and heard Mrs. Tilton call out: "Dory Tilton, why don't you come to bed? It's after twelve o'clock. What are you running around in your nightclothes for?" This peculiarity of nocturnal picture-hanging was surpassed, Bessie recounted, by Tilton's habit of switching around at night from bed to bed in a petulant effort to find one the softness of which suited him. These excursions through the house would usually occur in summer, when he would go around "from one bed to another, trying all the beds in the house before he could make up his mind." Sometimes this could be inconvenient for others, including herself, Bessie emphasized. She described one occasion when Mr. and Mrs. Tilton "had gone to bed in the second-story back bedroom, and I was sleeping in the room next to theirs, the back bedroom, and the first thing I knew, here he came, saying, 'Pettie, let us go in and try Bessie's bed a little while.' Mrs. Tilton was behind him with a pillow, and . . . I went upstairs in the third-story back bedroom, and I hadn't been up there five minutes, just long enough to get into bed, before he says, 'Pettie, suppose we try this bed a little while, perhaps this is the softest. That was three beds he had tried . . . and that night they slept in the front bedroom. That was four beds, and that was all the beds there was in the house."

Bessie's tales of Tilton were climaxed by charges that he made overtures to her. She eventually told this story with such detail, and clung to it, that millions of Americans were happily fortified in their belief that it was Tilton and not Beecher who was a cad; it scarcely seemed to matter, even if what Bessie said was so, and hers was the only testimony on the subject, that the adultery charge against the preacher might also be true, and that it was far more substantiated. Nevertheless, what Bessie charged not only took the edge off what Theodore Tilton charged Beecher with, but also provided one of the most intimate and amusing moments in the scandal.

One night in 1867, Bessie related, "I had not been in bed very long before Mr. Tilton came in and said he had come to kiss me good-night. I was lying on the side of the bed next the door. He went around on the other side and leaned over and kissed me . . . He stroked my forehead and my hair, and said what nice soft hair I had, and how nice and soft my flesh was—my forehead, and then he put his hand, was putting his hand, in my neck, and I took his hand out. And he says 'Why, Bessie, my dear, you are painfully modest.' He says, 'Why, those caresses, those are all right. People in the best society do all those things, and it is perfectly proper. Nobody but people that had impure minds think of such things as that as not being right.' And I said I could not help what they did in the best class of society, that I had my own ideas of what was proper and what was modest, and I was going to carry them out. If I didn't think it was proper for him to put his hand in my neck, I was not going to let him do it . . . He then laid down and asked me if I did not—if I would not—like to be married, I ought to have a good husband. I said that I supposed when the time came—the right man came along—perhaps I would get married. But I didn't think getting married was the chief end aim in life. It didn't trouble me very much, and that if I was married there was one thing very sure, I didn't think I would ever have a literary man for a husband. And then he asked me if I didn't think some people had affinities for each other. Well, I asked him what he meant by that, what he meant by 'affinities,' and he said that when a man saw a woman that he loved she should be his affinity and they should live together as man and wife, that was what he meant. And then he went on to say that if I would allow him to caress me and to love me as he wanted to do that no harm should come to me, and that a physical expression of love was just the same as a kiss or a caress. He then went on to describe again—to tell that he knew ministers that caressed girls and married women; it was all perfectly all right and proper and beautiful. And then he told me that I was a very strange child. He says, 'Bessie, you have some very singular ideas,' and kissed me good-night, and left."

Bessie's story may have been rambling, but it sounded convincing. Tilton denied as "pure fiction" everything she said about him, including a further account of having once carried her while she was asleep from her bed to his and having on several occasions, in her presence, wildly accused Mrs. Tilton

ELIZABETH A. TURNER

of adultery with three other friends of the family. There was, however, a graphic quality to what she said that bolstered the belief it was more than a product of a young girl's imagination, even though her sympathies from the start were clearly with Mrs. Tilton. There was a strong suspicion, too, that before she came to testify, she was coached by Beecher's friends to impute to Tilton, retroactively, the exact language and amorous reasoning he publicly pinned on the wooing pastor.

Whether Tilton's sins were of the body or of the soul, it was a fact that he was constrained by his lecturing to be as continuously absent as he was forever penitent in his letters home. And whatever his consolations, his steady moving-about precluded the kind of constant, solicitous companionship Henry Ward Beecher could afford Elizabeth Tilton. Even when he was bestowing it, however, Beecher had his own forms of torment. Back in 1861, when Lucy Maria Bowen's passion had proved too much for him to handle, and he had found it necessary to put an end to the relationship, he had written: "The consciousness of being loved . . . always produces a reaction in every generous nature. It produces a sense of unworthiness, it produces sadness, and a sense of sinfulness and inefficiency." In spite of the convenience of his modern, flexible creed, Beecher's old Calvinist past, as he had inherited even the tempered version from his father, kept rising up to haunt him. The ordeal of trying to avoid a new crisis with Lib Tilton came to be a struggle for him as well as for her. Beecher always made things harder by arguing with himself in public. Theodore Tilton, he intimated one Sunday, was not the only one who dealt in "affinities." From his pulpit, the preacher intoned that "as men grow toward love, finer and finer are those interpreting sympathies by which they select . . . those that by elective affinity are theirs by purity, by capacity, by self-denial." Way back, when he was still out West, Beecher had preached a famous sermon against adulterers and their wickedness, and in his early days in Brooklyn he had proclaimed that "excuses for moral delinquency . . . are processes of self-deception" and that "nothing is more common than that men may . . . with a certain kind of exterior morality

[make] themselves noticeably good in external matters while they have actually lost the power of moral discrimination in respect to their own inward habits."

Poor Elizabeth Tilton, who was always ready to swoon when she listened to Beecher preach, felt her capacity for self-denial dwindle day by day. The fact that both she and Theodore, in the letters they continued frantically to exchange, could share for a moment their disappointment over some of Beecher's political activities, such as his support of President Johnson's restoration policy that seemed too easily to forgive the sins of Southern slavery, was not enough to restrain her love for the pastor. "There is no spot so sacred on all this earth as Plymouth Church," she wrote Tilton, begging him to return and fulfill his vows again, which she coupled with her own struggle for purity and abnegation. The struggle grew hopeless.

By this time, in 1867, Beecher had paid her the highest compliment: sharing a creative problem with her. Under contract for the record sum of $24,000 to write a novel for Robert Bonner's highly successful New York Ledger, he was having his troubles. He envied the talent for fiction of his sister, Mrs. Stowe, and what he had to do was especially difficult as he had agreed to write the novel serially so a chapter could be released each week to a breathless public. Beecher couldn't get started. He kept writing pages and tearing them up, and he told Bonner, fitfully: "I have dreamed two plots, but forgot them as soon as I waked!" Finally, after applying various "coaxing" techniques to himself, he finished a few chapters. But, as he put it, "I was about in despair, and I needed somebody or other that would not be critical, and that would praise it, to give me the courage to go on with it." Eunice Beecher was no help, but if there was a person on earth who would fill the prescription, it was Elizabeth Tilton.

He took the manuscript over to Livingston Street and read parts of it aloud to her. "She was good enough to speak very enthusiastically of them," he said, "and was particularly delighted with that scene in which the heroine was born, when the old doctor had gone out into the fields and gathered a crown of trailing arbutus." Beecher had written of this flower:

> It is like the breath of love. The pure white and pink blossoms in sweet clusters lie hidden under leaves or grass, and often under untimely snows. Blessings on thee! Thou art the fairest, most modest, and sweetest-breathed of all our flowers!

Norwood was described as "a New England idyll," and a short time later, on a trip to Boston, Beecher by chance found a picture called "The Trailing Arbutus." He promptly bought it and lugged it back to Brooklyn for Lib Tilton, who proudly displayed it to Susan Anthony and other visitors.

When Beecher read her a section of the novel which dealt with the romantic thoughts of Rose Wentworth, the heroine, toward her husband, and which included the passage:

> It would seem as if, while her whole life centered upon his love, she would hide the precious secret by flinging over it vines and flowers, by mirth and raillery, as a bird hides its nest under tufts of grass, and behind leaves and vines, as a fence against prying eyes. . .

Elizabeth Tilton was more than honored. She felt blessed by a divine approbation that had made her, in Beecher's eyes, the incarnation of Rose Wentworth herself. She remembered the image later, when she had come to feel the full weight of her guilt, and wrote to him that her weapons had been "love, a large untiring generosity, and *nest-hiding*!" Lib Tilton was always to underline the most embarrassing words.

The winter of 1867—was a cold and nasty one. On the 20th of February, Mrs. Tilton wrote her husband in the West one of those tormented letters:

> MY BELOVED: I am so lonesome and heartsick for your companionship tonight that I hesitate to write lest my

mood depress you. Yet I cannot wish you home, for I am persuaded you are happier where you are. While I long to be with you, I am haunted continually with fears that your cheery face will soon be shadowed and the dear head droop! This thought is agony to me, and I have spent many hours since your absence weeping because of it . . . I would fain make the path smooth for your feet, or in other words direct the children and the household that they minister harmony only, but I *know* I cannot, and *I am afraid*!

"'Good angels guard thy sleep,'" Elizabeth said at the end of this one, which she signed "Wifey," but once again the underlining spoke for itself. The coming of the good weather only brought more trouble, and then tragedy. In August, Mrs. Tilton's son Paul died of cholera. Beecher came down from his farm in Peekskill to preach at the funeral. Tilton had hardly got to know his baby, he had been away so much. Mrs. Tilton dwelt heavily on Paul's death all through the long and difficult summer. When her husband took the road again that fall, she kept mostly to herself. But on Friday, October 9, she resolved to come out of her funk. Beecher was making a speech in support of President Grant at the Brooklyn Academy of Music. It was one of his most impassioned, and, as usual, Lib Tilton, who got dressed specially for the occasion and sat in one of the front rows, thought him magnificent. The next afternoon, brimming with admiration but full of fresh sorrow over the death of Paul because he would never have the chance to hear Beecher, she went to see her pastor at his home on Columbia Heights. He was alone, writing his sermon for the next day, somewhat ahead of his usual last-minute schedule. His family was up on the farm.

The language of the complaint Theodore Tilton eventually brought in City Court, Brooklyn, made the charge of what took place explicit:

That the defendant, contriving and willfully intending to injure the plaintiff and deprive him of the comfort, society, aid and assistance of the said Elizabeth, the wife of the plaintiff, and to alienate and destroy her affection for him, heretofore on or about the tenth day of October, 1868, and on diverse other days and times after that day and before the commencement of this action, at the house of the defendant, No. 124 Columbia Street, City of Brooklyn, and at the house of the plaintiff, No. 174 Livingston Street, City of Brooklyn, wrongfully and wickedly and without the privity or connivance of the plaintiff, debauched and carnally knew the said Elizabeth, then and ever since the wife of the plaintiff, by means whereof the affection of the said Elizabeth for the said plaintiff was wholly alienated and destroyed; and by reason of the premises the plaintiff has wholly lost the comfort, society, aid and assistance of his said wife, which during all the time aforesaid he otherwise might and ought to have had and enjoyed.

There was never to be, in the vast correspondence of confession and denial that followed, any further description of the time or place of actual acts of adultery beyond the fact, also charged by Tilton, that a week later, at the Tilton home, a second intimate embrace occurred. He was to be sustained in court, before the trial began, that a bill of particulars was not required. Nor was what Elizabeth Tilton wrote in her diary ever to be made public, beyond a single entry. Under the date of October 10, 1868, she wrote: "A Day Memorable."

Beecher kept no diary, but the pulpit frequently served him as his confessional. Several weeks after the "memorable" day, he preached on sin. "The man who has been wallowing in lust, the man who has been on fire in his passions, and who by God's great goodness has been brought to an hour and a moment when, with the lurid light of revelation, his monstrous wickedness stands disclosed in him—that man ought not to wait so long as the drawing of his breath," he said. "Wherever he is, no matter how decorous his audience may be, if he does the thing that is safest and best he will rise in his place and make

BEECHER'S THEORY AND PRACTICE

H.W.B.—"The man who can't live on bread and water is not fit to live!"

confession. Though it be in church, and it break the order and routine of service, he will stand up and say, 'Here I am, a sinner, and I confess my sin, and I call on God to witness my determination from this hour to turn away from it.' That is the wise course, and you would think so—if it was anybody else but yourself."

It was typical of Beecher to stand off in this fashion and regard himself, to formulate his own tangled rationale and make of it a pragmatic homily. If he managed some kind of subconscious exculpation, he apparently considered it applicable to the future. In five weeks during the early part of 1869, when Tilton was once more away, Beecher paid Lib Tilton twelve pastoral calls. They went shopping together and he bought her a variety of gifts Tilton later discovered locked in a closet. They included perfumes, fancy soaps, stationery, and a collection of photographs of Beecher in various poses, a picture of Mary holding the body of Christ, and copies of Beecher's books, among them a new edition of his *Sermons* and a volume of *The Life of Jesus, the Christ*, which Elizabeth had helped him edit— Beecher described it as "entering into her life, and, in a sense, giving her an interest in mine."

During the spring of 1870, Tilton was again absent and Beecher took Lib Tilton driving in his buggy; he owned a pair of spanking grays and loved to drive fast. Their intimacy now, according to what Mrs. Tilton was shortly to tell her husband, was infrequent, though Beecher was always persistent. Some time this spring, sick of mind and body and no longer as convinced as she had been by Beecher's assurances that their relations were divine and proper, she left somewhat earlier than usual for Schoharie, N.Y., to pass the hot months as usual. When she returned suddenly to Livingston Street on the night of July 3, she went immediately to her bedroom on the second floor. This was the same room in which little Paul had died two years before, and it was here that her famous confession to her husband took place.

CHAPTER IV

Only one person was ever to give a thorough account of what Elizabeth Tilton told Theodore Tilton on this hot night in July. That person was Theodore Tilton.

Mrs. Tilton was subsequently to explain and re-explain her actions and behavior many times and in many different ways in an ever more complicated and futile effort to protect Beecher, her husband, herself and the way of life that revolved around Plymouth Church. She would never succeed in clearing her conscience, however, and by the time it drove her to a final confrontation of herself, her long record of erratic statements simply sustained those who had always wanted to believe her innocent—the argument then being that her guilt remained unproved simply because she could no longer be believed in anything she said. Her final reckoning would not come for eight years from this muggy evening, and its effect then, beyond being anti-climactic, would but adumbrate the whole saga of rationalization the Beecher-Tilton case provoked.

The interview with his wife was to be related by Tilton on several occasions, but most completely in court. While he, too, was to dedicate himself for some time to secrecy and protection, and would offer different versions of what Elizabeth had confessed, his final explanations had a quality of consistence that her ceaseless affirmations and denials lacked. She began her tragic unburdening, he said on the witness stand, with great "womanly feeling," announcing that she had come back to Brooklyn from the country "to communicate to me a secret which had long been resting on her mind." She had tried on several occasions to "throw off" the tormenting knowledge in her heart but "had not been brought quite to the point of courage to make the disclosure." Before she gave the facts, Tilton said, "she exacted from me a pledge that I would do no harm to the person concerning whom the secret was to be told." She also made him promise "not to communicate to the person the fact that she had made such a revelation to me, because, as she said, she wished to inform him of that revelation herself."

He thereupon heard his wife's recitation, which he retold with such detail and narrative flow that it surely marked him, even in the minds of his detractors, as a good reporter, whether of fact or fancy. He continued:

> She then said to me that it was a secret between herself and the Rev. Henry Ward Beecher, her pastor; that, as I was well aware, there had been, during a long course of years, a friendship between herself and her pastor; that this friendship, contrary to my expectation or belief, had been in later years more than friendship; that it had been love; that it had been more than love, it had been sexual intimacy; that this sexual intimacy had begun shortly after the death of her son Paul; that she had been in a tender frame of mind, consequent upon that bereavement; that she had received much consolation during that shadow on our house, from her pastor; that she had made a visit to his house while she was still suffering from that sorrow, and that there, on the 10th of October, 1868, she had surrendered her body to him in sexual embrace; that she had repeated such an act on the following Saturday evening at her own residence, 174 Livingston Street; that she had consequent upon those two occasions repeated such acts at various times, at his

residence and at hers, and at other places—such acts of sexual intercourse continuing from the Fall of 1868 to the Spring of 1870.

Mrs. Tilton, according to what Tilton further said, set forth her motivations clearly, always emphasizing that they had been as religious as they had been physical. His story of what she told him went on:

That she had in the early stages of their friendship [Mr. Beecher's and hers] been greatly distressed at rumors concerning Mr. Beecher's moral integrity; that she had wished to show that there was a woman who was superior to the silly flatteries with which many ladies in his congregation had courted his society; that she wished to demonstrate the honor and the dignity of her sex; that she had done so in her own thought, until finally she had been persuaded by him that, as their love was proper and not wrong, therefore it followed that any expression of that love, whether by the shake of the hand or the kiss of the lips, or even bodily intercourse, since it was all an expression of that which by itself was not wrong, therefore that bodily intercourse was not wrong; that Mr. Beecher had professed to her a greater love than he had ever shown to any woman in his life; that she and I both knew that for years his home had not been a happy one; that his wife had not been a satisfactory wife to him; that she wished—that he wished to find in her—Elizabeth—the consolation, the help to his mind, and the solace of life which had been denied to him by the unfortunate marriage at home; that he had made these arguments to her during the early years of their friendship, and she had steadfastly resisted; that he had many times fondled her to the degree that it required on her part almost bodily resistance to be rid of him; that after her final surrender, in October, 1868, he had then many times solicited her when she had refused; that the occasions of her yielding her body to him had not been numerous, but that his solicitations had been frequent and urgent, and sometimes almost violent; that she had made this confession to me because the sense of deceitfulness in her mind was a pain to her conscience . . . that she never could look me honestly in the face again until she had made a full and free confession.

Tilton believed his wife from the outset when she said she had never been unfaithful "out of vulgar thoughts," that she had been prompted throughout by "pure affection and a high religious love." As he put it, she gave no evidence "that the great fact which she had confessed was wrong, but that the wrong which she wished to throw from her mind was mainly the necessary deceit with which she had hitherto concealed it from her husband." To a friend of his, George Alfred Townsend, one of the best-known journalists of the day, who wrote as "Gath," Tilton was to declare: "I think she sinned her sin as one in a trance. I don't think she was a free agent. I think she would have done his bidding if, like the heathen-priest in the Hindoo-land, he had bade her fling her child into the Ganges or cast herself under the Juggernaut."

Contrary to what she had imagined had been his "expectations and belief," the thought of his wife's adultery had been lurking at the back of Tilton's mind (Elizabeth's own letters had certainly shown an awareness of such suspicions). Nevertheless, the actual recital of it left Tilton "just blasted." As he told Townsend: "Both of us spent the night alone in the midst of this nightmare. In the morning I went early to my office in the *Brooklyn Union* building, but I could not write. I felt that I must come to some determination." His response to his soul-searching was that "I must find some excuse for her—other people might blame, but I must pardon her, and I found that excuse in the fact that she had been trapped up in her teacher and guide, she had surrendered her convictions to him, she had followed his beck and lead trustingly, she would go after him like one blinded," and "at last I said, 'That man is growing old, I will punish him only to this extent—Elizabeth shall go and tell him that I know from her own lips which pattern of Godliness he is, and that I am living, suffering sacrifice for his children as well as my own.'" Having thus decided to be "in my secret self a conqueror," Tilton explained to Townsend that "for two weeks I lived a kind of ecstasy; I walked the streets as if I scarcely touched the ground, and the greatness of temptation I had put away, the magnanimity of the life I was leading, the sacrifice, made me radiant, so that I wrote without labor."

Among the things he wrote, perhaps as an unconscious sop to himself, was a strange editorial called "The Wreck of a Life" in the *Independent*:

> When a man of unusually fine organization, with high-strung nerves, with a supersensitive conscience, with a tremendous sensibility to reputation, and with a boundless ambition, suddenly, by one act, sacrifices the slow honors of a lifetime, there is something in his self-destruction to excite the pity of mankind . . . He can never again be his former self . . . Every day's sunshine will mock him, and make him see the shadows of his soul. No bird will ever sing in his ear without reviving his innocence as a memory and his guilt as a fact. He is like one who has lived his appointed span. The grave awaits him. Death is his next friend.

It was doubtful that anyone caught the allusion, least of all Beecher himself. He hardly ever read the *Independent* any more, now that he was so busy with his own publication, the *Christian Union*, and for most of July and August he was up on the farm at Peekskill.

Lib Tilton had meanwhile gone back to Schoharie. Despite her resolve herself to tell Beecher about her confession and thereby bury the past completely, her courage had failed her. Early in August, however, she again returned to the house on Livingston Street. Tilton was away, and she summoned her pastor at once. He rushed down from Peekskill. "I found her lying

CURIOUS RUSTICS OGLE BEECHER AT THE PEEKSKILL STATION

in the upstairs, second-story front room," he recalled. She was on a sofa, "and she seemed to me like one who wanted to talk and didn't. I prayed with her and cheered her as best I could." In their prayers, it was later indicated, they jointly invoked God's aid to keep their sexual intimacy ended. But Lib Tilton failed as before—she was unable to tell Beecher, to warn him, that she had unburdened herself to her husband. The preacher called again the next day, but she was too upset even to see him and sent a girl down with a note that "all would be all right, or something, in the future," as Beecher was to recollect it. He took the train back to Peekskill, and shortly after went to the White Mountains, where he stayed two months each year to allay his hay fever, and where all summer long he remained blissfully unaware that, the secret of his "nest-hiding" was out.

Back in the steaming city, Tilton was left to brood alone. In spite of the pledge of silence he had taken, his wife's confession worked away at him. One morning he went to see an old friend, Martha Bradshaw, a deaconess of Plymouth Church and one of the best-known and most respected women on Brooklyn

Heights, and he told her the story. Mrs. Tilton kept moving back and forth between the country and the city, her sorrow and nervousness abetted by pregnancy. She and Tilton scarcely spoke, but she, too, soon felt that she had to talk to someone. Guests at the Tiltons' had come to be invited less frequently, but among the visitors who still came were Miss Anthony, Mrs. Stanton, and Mrs. Bullard, the three feminist leaders with whom Mrs. Tilton had maintained her vague association in certain phases of the fight for women's rights before her private troubles overcame her.

One evening in the fall Mrs. Bullard and Mrs. Stanton went out to dinner with Tilton. He was supposed to have stopped off at home to pick up Miss Anthony, who was keeping the ailing Mrs. Tilton company, but he somehow forgot. Over the dinner table, Tilton told Mrs. Stanton and Mrs. Bullard of the influence of Beecher in his household. He railed against the pastor. "Oh, that the damned lecherous scoundrel should have defiled my bed . . . and at the same time professed to be my best friend," he cried. "Had he come to me like a man and confessed his guilt, I could perhaps have ignored it, but to have him creep like a snake into my house, leaving his pollution behind him, and I so blind as not to see, and esteeming him all the while as a saint, Oh, it is too much!" Mrs. Stanton later commented: "I never saw such a manifestation of mental agony."

At eleven o'clock Tilton returned home alone. Mrs. Tilton's later account of what then took place became a vital part of the lengthy conspiracy to reduce the severity of the scandal, an often fantastic effort to make it appear that the pastor had simply made "unhandsome advances" to her—a peculiar face-saving device even Tilton for a time was willing to accept—or that there had been nothing more than unrequited lovesick adulation on her part. Since this campaign, chiefly to protect Beecher, would make it advisable to limit the number of persons who might have been told of the actual adultery, Mrs. Tilton in time had to deny some of her early confessions, including one she apparently made during this night in 1870 to Miss Anthony.

Lib Tilton's story was that when Tilton appeared, Miss Anthony rebuked him for not returning earlier, that he grew angry, and that after fleeing to an upstairs bedroom in self-protection Miss Anthony recounted to her some of Tilton's sins of unfaithfulness. Before a Plymouth Church committee, Mrs. Tilton was to temper this by saying that at most she might have *repeated* Tilton's charges against her, believing that Miss Anthony, as a "reasonable person," would not believe them. But it appeared that Miss Anthony had believed them, for the next day she went out to Tenafly, New Jersey, where Mrs. Stanton lived. She told Mrs. Stanton that she had acted as Mrs. Tilton's protector when Theodore and Elizabeth almost came to blows, and that she had locked herself in the room, announcing to the enraged husband through the bolted barricade that he would enter only over her own dead body. Mrs. Stanton, who became a sort of historian of the occasion, eventually told the rest. "Mrs. Tilton remained with Susan throughout the night," she said, "and in the excitement of the hour, amid sobs and tears, she told all to Miss Anthony, the whole story of her own faithlessness, of Mr. Beecher's course, of her deception and of her anguish. We compared notes and found that by both man and wife the same story had been told." Mrs. Bullard corroborated it.

Lib Tilton's next mistake, her biggest, was to tell the story of her sinning to her mother, Mrs. Morse, who was to be chiefly responsible for tattling it around town. Tilton's appraisal of his mother-in-law was not prejudiced, according to those who knew her. "This eccentric lady has for years been animated by violent hatreds and an uncontrollable temper, resulting often in hysterical fits," he said. He described her as "a chronic subject of manias and frenzies" who once grabbed Mr. Morse, her second husband, "and strangled him 'till he grew black in the face,'" her grasp having "to be loosened with difficulty by the inmates of the house, and her fury quenched with chloroform, a circumstance speedily followed by a legal separation between her husband and herself." There had even been talk about putting Mrs. Morse in an asylum. When she was not having one of her fits of "insane hysterics" and acting "cunning and malicious in the extreme," Tilton said, she was capable of "innate kindliness and beautiful affection of nature"; but it was something he seldom profited by personally, for Mrs. Morse hated him. She thoroughly disapproved of his friends and his ideas, from Susan Anthony to Abolitionism, and she thought he wasted his time and his money on them.

Mrs. Morse had lived with the Tiltons until a year or so prior to Mrs. Tilton's confession. The occasion of her departure had been one of her most violent attacks of madness. "Twice she thrust her parasol like a rapier in my breast, breaking off the handle," Tilton said. Then she came at him with a carving knife and threatened to cut his heart out. "Unable to endure this treatment with equanimity," as Tilton put it, he and his wife agreed that for the safety and well-being of all concerned, her mother ought to go. She took a little house near by on Brooklyn Heights, but her influence on Livingston Street, despite the fact that Tilton had forbidden her to enter his home, was still felt. Now, when she heard her daughter's awful tale, she began to formulate a little plot of her own to get rid of Tilton. Visualizing Henry Ward Beecher as the permanent protector of her daughter and herself, if Tilton could somehow be eliminated, she went so far as to privately consult a divorce lawyer, "a fact which we learned only by accident," Tilton said, "not until it had spread its bat's-wings and gone flying abroad." She wrote anonymous letters to Tilton's newspaper friends, relating, with "her mischief-making propensities," a long list of his cruelties toward herself and his wife. Tilton soon began receiving a flow of vituperative letters from his mother-in-law. "You infernal villain!" they would start out. "This night you should be in jail . . . Your slimy, polluted, brawny hand curses everything you touch. . ." There was to be no stopping Mrs. Morse, not even when she sat down and started writing letters to Beecher with the salutation "My Dear Son."

In her plot to undo Tilton, Mrs. Morse enlisted the aid of two others. One of them was Bessie Turner, the adopted girl in the Tilton household, whose tales of Tilton's idiosyncrasies and attentions to her, whether true or false to degree, were surely prompted in part by Mrs. Morse's urging. The other was Eunice Beecher, "whose peculiarities, having less aggravation," Tilton was to write, "are also less pardonable than Mrs. Morse's." It was now eleven years since Tilton and Mrs. Beecher had spoken. "I have never had so relentless an enemy," he said. She had neither forgiven him for being the only one who had been able, through his influence in Washington, to save her son from disgrace during the war, nor for his long-time influence over her husband. Beecher's turning from his own house to enjoy the favors and friendships he found at the Tiltons' now aggravated her distaste for the hot causes Tilton propounded, which so distressed and embarrassed her Puritan soul.

Late in October 1870, Lib Tilton in despair fled to friends in Marietta, Ohio, from where she sent her husband what was tantamount to a written version of her earlier oral confession—a letter that would prove hard to disavow:

> When, by your threats, my mother cried out to me, 'Why, what have you done, Elizabeth, my child?' her worst suspicions were aroused, and I laid bare my heart then, that from my lips, and not yours, she might receive the dagger into her heart . . . For the agony which the revelation has caused *you*, my cries ascend to Heaven night and day that upon mine own head all the anguish may fall . . . Even so, every word, look or intimation against Mr. B., though I be in no wise brought in, is an agony beyond the piercing of myself a hundred times. His position and his good name are dear to me. Once again I implore you, for your children's sake, to whom you have a duty in this matter, that *my past* be buried— left with me and my God.

Bessie Turner had gone out to Ohio with Mrs. Tilton, and on the 9th of November they returned. Almost at once another bitter argument took place between the Tiltons, according to Bessie, in which she, pledging herself to stand by Mrs. Tilton, received from Tilton "a terrible blow that hurled me to the opposite side of the room." When this later came to be told in court, Tilton denied all of it, but comely Bessie's account was listened to raptly. "He came forward, perfectly bland— you would think nothing in the world had ever happened—so composed and so calm," she said. "'Why,' he says, 'why, Bessie, my dear, you tripped and fell, didn't you?' I turned around to him, said I, 'Theodore Tilton, are you a fool, or do you take me for one?'" In her presence, Bessie said, Tilton pointed to a red lounge and said it had been "consecrated to sexual intercourse" between his wife and Beecher. The next morning Mrs. Tilton and Bessie packed and went off to Mrs. Morse's, but Tilton followed them later in the day and begged Elizabeth to return home, which she did, to Mrs. Morse's intense dissatisfaction. Bessie gave a good description of that irascible lady. "Mrs. Morse was coming down the stairs," she said, "and Mr. Tilton looked up and said, 'Good evening, Grandma.' Mrs. Morse said, 'I will grandma you, you perfidious wretch, you infernal hypocrite, you most miserable scoundrel!' and he said, 'Why, Grandma, you seem to be so excited,' and she says, 'Oh, you infernal scoundrel, I will publish you from Dan to Beersheba.'" It was a good example of Mrs. Morse's abomination of her son-in-law.

In a few days Mrs. Morse struck again. She sent Bessie Turner around to see Henry Ward Beecher and told her to give the preacher a full story of Tilton's harsh behavior toward his wife and of his nocturnal prowlings. Beecher was "shocked." As he later recalled it, "She called upon me, I should think, about the middle of the forenoon, and said that she was requested to ask that I go down and see Mrs. Tilton at her mother's house, that she had left her husband and did not intend to return." Beecher asked Bessie what had happened. "She told me that she had seen him treating his wife with great rudeness and cruelty," he said. Modestly, and with a downcast look, Bessie also told him about Tilton's alleged improprieties with her, the pastor added.

He went around to Mrs. Morse's place, where he found both Mrs. Tilton and her mother waiting for him. Mrs. Morse did most of the talking, and what she told him of Tilton's "despotism" seemed "like a nightmare dream" to Beecher. In her "practical, incisive, and earnest way," he said, Mrs. Morse told him "that her daughter had lived a life of great unhappiness, that she was subject to great cruelty and deprivation, and that her life with Mr. Tilton had become intolerable." Beecher pondered a moment, and then said: "This is a case in which I feel that a man can't give the best counsel. It is a case, it seems to me, where a woman is needed, and if you will allow me I shall be glad to bring my wife and let her hear, for I think much of her judgment about such things." Mrs. Morse jumped at the offer. "I will bless her, if she will come, as long as I live," she said.

The next day Beecher brought Eunice with him to Mrs. Morse's house. First Mrs. Beecher and Elizabeth Tilton went upstairs to talk, and then Mrs. Morse and Mrs. Beecher had a session. It was the first time in several months that Beecher and Mrs. Tilton had been left alone together. "She was very despondent," Beecher later thought. "How is it," he said he asked, "that I have been so long with you and you never alluded before to me about distress in your household?" She replied, according to the pastor, that she had sought to conceal her troubles in the hope they would pass away. "I recollect saying to her that I thought with the blessing of God she would be able to see the light yet," Beecher was to say. "I joined with her in prayer—the most of the time I was with her, I was praying to let patience have its perfect work." Once again Elizabeth had not been able to get herself to tell Beecher the truth, that she had confessed their intimacy to her husband.

The following day, after he had talked it over with his wife, Beecher signed a scrap of paper and handed it to Eunice. "I incline to think that your view is right," he wrote, "and that a separation and settlement of support will be wisest." Mrs. Beecher took it over to Mrs. Morse's for Mrs. Tilton to consider. But Lib Tilton did not follow the suggestion of the Beechers. She went back to her own home on Livingston Street, at her lowest ebb. During the next few weeks her husband was seldom at the house. He often slept at the home of a friend over on Remsen Street, Frank De Pau Moulton, a wealthy importer and man about town who was destined henceforth to play a major role in the great scandal. "Night after night, I walked with my waterproof cloak on, and would go back and creep into the basement and lie down anywhere, feeling utterly miserable," Elizabeth was to say later. The house was without fire and the servants hardly gave her enough to eat, not that she felt like eating. One day she went out to Greenwood Cemetery, where two of her children by now were buried, and lay down on their graves until the keeper ordered her off.

On the 24th of December, Mrs. Tilton suffered a miscarriage and took to her bed. Some time later, to a friend, she bemoaned the loss of this child. "A love-babe, it promised, you know," she wrote, cryptically. It was to become part of the gossip of the day that Lib Tilton's baby was aborted, with the assistance of her mother and at least the knowledge of Henry Ward Beecher, though not of his wife.

PART 2

THE OVERTURNED NEST

CHAPTER V

It was at this point in the great scandal that Henry Bowen, the publisher, stimulated by the tales of Tilton's mischievous mother-in-law, Mrs. Morse, played a decisive and Machiavellian role. As was almost always the case, the fates seemed to conspire against Theodore Tilton, so that a combination of personal and public misfortunes brought him into deep water with the man he could least afford to offend, his employer. By his foolish and headstrong behavior, Tilton became a perfect foil for Bowen's plotting.

The two men, by the fall of 1870, had begun to have certain differences. There was, first of all, a small matter of graft. One of Bowen's friends, who was a crony of President Grant's, had been serving as Collector of the Port of New York. The "general order business" of the port had provided one of the choicest bits of graft in the whole sorry history of the Grant administration. Just how much Henry Bowen was involved was not known, but he made it quite clear to Tilton, who by now was directing both of his papers, the *Independent* and the *Union*, that he wanted his journals to come to Grant's support. Tilton flatly refused. Bowen then demanded that Tilton write editorials in support of a man he wanted to become the Republican Congressman from Brooklyn. Tilton again refused. For fifteen years Bowen had given his young editor his head; but now Bowen rebelled. There was only one way, he surmised aloud, for him to obtain the backing he wanted for his candidate, and that was by dismissing his editor. "Yes, but that is the only way," Tilton proudly replied. Whatever faults Tilton had, a lack of principles was not one of them.

Bowen was not sure that he wanted to risk a public breach with Tilton in which his own moral position would not be the soundest; but there were other reasons why he was disturbed about his editor. In his leaders for the *Independent*, Tilton had been making increasingly clear his feelings against stringent divorce laws. He had also acquired a passion he kept proclaiming in print for French poetry and philosophy. Rumblings in Church circles had spread from the East to the West, where a group of clerical champions of the *status quo*, including one of Beecher's brothers, had already complained. On the 1st of December, 1870, Tilton had written one of his longest and most ardent editorials under the general heading of "Love, Marriage and Divorce." It had contained what seemed some pretty startling statements:

Marriage without love is a sin against God—a sin which, like other sins, is to be repented of, ceased from and put away. No matter with what solemn ceremony the twain may have been made one, yet, when love departs, then marriage ceases, and divorce begins. This is the essence of Christ's idea. To say that He granted divorce only for a gross and fleshly crime is to forget that He called the eye a paramour and the heart of wanton's bed. Even granting that one of His speeches seems to call adultery the only divorce, yet in His other maxims He illustrates what He meant by adultery. He set forth an ideal of so faithful a fidelity that most marriages estimated by this standard would be proved adulterous and be pronounced by His withering judgment null and void . . . Marriage, if it be marriage at all, is the unswerving faithfulness of husband and wife, admitting no intervening mistress for the one, no supplemental paramour for the other. But this idea . . . carries with it as its logical sequence . . . the irresistible conclusion that marriage, if broken, and whether broken by the body or the soul, is divorce.

There may not have been much in that with which Eunice Beecher, could she have read it in the solitude of her heart's reflection, would have disagreed; except that, knowing that love had gone out of her life, if it had ever been there at all, she would have been the last to let herself be led from the bitter safety of her own sorrow to the divorce court. As for Tilton, it would have taken a battery of modern-day psychoanalysts to separate the strings of his subconscious. But whatever impelled him, his own words were surely self-intoxicating. In a lighter vein, he wrote and published a poem which showed that his own romantic faith was still not completely soured by the unhappy developments in his household. It was called "French With a Master—A New Poem By Theodore Tilton," and its repeated theme, *"Aimer, aimer, c'est a vivre"* was printed at the top and translated, somewhat awkwardly, as "To love, to love, this is it to live." A few verses read:

Teach you French? I will, my dear!
Sit down and con your lesson here.
What did Adam say to Eve?
Aimer, aimer, c'est a vivre.

French is always spoken best
Breathing deeply from the chest;
Darling, does your bosom heave?
Aimer, aimer, c'est a vivre.

Tell me, may I understand
When I press your little hand,
That our hearts together cleave?
Aimer, aimer, c'est a vivre.

Or, if I presume too much,
Teaching French by sense of touch,
Grant me pardon and reprieve!
Aimer, aimer, c'est a vivre.

It is possible that if Tilton deserved to be fired at all, he deserved it more for his poetry than his prose, but Henry Bowen first sought another way to limit the ready flow of his pen. He offered Tilton a new contract. It did not matter too much, he now figured, if the *Union* at least stayed neutral about certain political matters; it might even be wiser. It would not do, however, for the *Independent*, still one of the biggest money-makers in the country despite the rise of Henry Ward Beecher's *Christian Union*, to get a bad name. So Bowen took over the editorship of the religious weekly himself, keeping Tilton as a contributor, and let Tilton continue to edit the *Brooklyn Union.*

The new arrangement, from a financial standpoint, suited Tilton admirably. It actually brought him, or was supposed to bring him, the most money Bowen had ever offered, $15,000 a year counting a share of the profits. If Bowen, in the back of his mind, had an idea that things might not work out, the sour-faced publisher carefully hid his intention. After the contracts had been drawn up, Tilton went around to the home of Oliver Johnson, an elderly associate on the *Independent*, and after telling Johnson about them, gave him a gold watch "as a parting tribute for the faithfulness with which he had toiled at my side." Thereupon Henry Bowen gave Tilton a gold watch to replace the one he had given away, and ran a tribute to Tilton in the next issue of the *Independent.* "Bold, uncompromising, a master among men; crisp, direct, earnest; brilliant, imaginative, poetic; keen as a Damascus blade and true as a needle to its pole in his sympathies with the needs of man, he was surely designed by Providence for the profession he has chosen," it said; even Bowen, once he got wound up, could render a fair version of the popular literary style.

It was all very polite and chummy until a few days before Christmas, when the effect of the tales told about Tilton by Mrs. Morse, and spread with the help of Mrs. Beecher, began reaching the open ears of Bowen. Tilton, his mother-in-law whispered, was about to abscond to Europe to join another woman. Bowen reported this and other stories about Tilton's alleged loose morals to Johnson, who for years had been patiently listening to Bowen's oft-repeated account of the sad chapter in the publisher's own past involving the adultery of Lucy Bowen with Henry Ward Beecher. When Bowen had declared that Beecher could be "driven from his pulpit and from Brooklyn in twelve hours," and when he had kept renewing his threats to do it, it had been Johnson who had helped hold him back. Now Johnson, to whom Tilton had recently confided his private sorrow and who had counseled patience and forgiveness in respect to that, too, advised Bowen to regard the rumors about Tilton tolerantly and with a grain of salt; Mrs. Morse, he pointed out, was not exactly a temperate, neutral source.

The next night, which was Christmas Eve, Johnson went around to Tilton's house to tell his young friend of Bowen's upset. Johnson later said Tilton admitted there had been one woman with whom he had had "very familiar relations—he said that he had been in bed with her in his own house," but that Tilton had denied the bulk of the rumors Bowen had heard about him, especially the story that he was planning to flee to France. On Monday the 26th of December, Bowen delivered, at his home on Willow Street and in Johnson's presence, what Tilton called "an avalanche of accusations . . . stories of immoralities, stories of atrocity . . . concerning my relations with women, and my drinking, and other things." Tilton agreed with Bowen that if the tales were true he ought not to live a day longer. "Mr. Bowen, bring here to me in your presence everybody who has anything against me, and let us have it out face to face," he said. Bowen agreed this was fair and then abruptly changed the subject. He told Tilton that he ought to give more space in the *Union* to affairs of Plymouth

Church and noted that Tilton had not even attended the church much lately. "I told him that I never again should cross the threshold of Plymouth Church," Tilton later recalled. "I then stated to him in a few words my wife's communication concerning Mr. Beecher."

Bowen thought quickly. He saw his chance finally to obtain his own revenge against Henry Ward Beecher. Here was a way to attack Beecher, through Tilton, without reviving and publicizing the sorry facts about Lucy Bowen and the preacher. Since he had remarried, the publisher had no wish to have that story come to the attention of his new wife. On the other hand, if Tilton failed in drawing the dagger, he could the more readily be fired for making the sensational accusation. If both men destroyed each other, so much the better.

Bowen thereupon launched forth into a tirade against Beecher. He called him "a wolf in the fold" and said he should be "extirpated" for having "shipwrecked Christian homes." Some of it, especially the sad tale of the seduction of Lucy Bowen, Tilton had heard, but there were new stories, including one that Beecher had taken a well-known authoress "by force, thrown her upon the sofa, and accomplished upon her his deviltry, then left her." When Bowen shouted: "You ought to proceed against him instantly!" Tilton asked why Bowen did not move himself. The publisher explained that Beecher had tearfully begged his pardon a year before, "and I cannot re-open a settled quarrel." But, he added, "if you will make a charge, I will furnish the proof . . . in the interest of morality and religion," and he promised to carry such a letter to Beecher, asseverating, "Mr. Beecher will not deny, cannot deny, dare not deny" the charges. As Tilton later summed it up, "Mr. Bowen put his case with such energy . . . and excited within me such a revived remembrance of the wrongs which Mr. Beecher had done to my own hearth, that I wrote a draft of a note which I altered and re-wrote and left finally changed as follows:

"December 26, 1870, Brooklyn
"Henry Ward Beecher:
"Sir: I demand that, for reasons which you explicitly
understand, you immediately cease from the ministry
of Plymouth Church, and that you quit the City of
Brooklyn as a residence.

"Theodore Tilton"

Henry Bowen put the unsealed letter in his pocket,
promising to deliver it during the afternoon. Tilton had
fallen neatly into the publisher's trap. He went on home,
and in an hour or so his friend Frank Moulton came by. He
told Moulton what he had done, and Moulton promptly
called him a ruined man and a fool. "Why didn't you get
his signature?" Moulton asked, and when Tilton said he
had believed Bowen's promise to furnish subsequent proof,
Moulton told him he should never have written the letter
in the first place. "You have left him a chance to play you
a trick," he added. "You have made your demand all alone.
What if he leaves you to support it all alone?" To protect
Tilton as best he could, Moulton sat down and wrote out
the following memorandum:

Brooklyn, Dec. 26, 1870.
T. T. informed me today that he had sent a note to Mr.
Beecher, of which Mr. H. C. Bowen was the bearer,
demanding that he (Mr. Beecher) should retire from
the pulpit and quit the City of Brooklyn. The letter was
an open one. H. C. Bowen knew the contents of it, and
said that he (Bowen) would sustain T. in the demand.
3.45 p.m.

It marked the beginning of the peculiar role Frank Moulton
was to play as human repository for the vast correspondence
that was to pour forth in the Beecher-Tilton case.

At five o'clock that gray day Henry Bowen dropped off
to see Beecher. He handed Beecher the note from Tilton

and watched carefully as the pastor read it; Beecher later claimed Bowen had said he was not aware of the contents, but Bowen himself never denied that he knew what the letter demanded. In either event, Beecher cried out: "Why, this man is crazy, this is sheer insanity!" At that sharp moment Henry Bowen decided that the preacher was either a remarkable actor or, as seemed far more likely, genuinely amazed. Quickly, the publisher reversed his field. He asked Beecher if there was any answer to be made to the letter. "Are you friendly with me, Mr. Bowen?" Beecher asked in turn. "I am," Bowen replied. "We have settled all our differences. I have no unfriendly feeling toward you. I come in no other way than as a friend."

For Theodore Tilton, as Frank Moulton had practically told him, it was the beginning of the end. Bowen and Beecher passed the rest of that dim afternoon exchanging gossip about him. According to Beecher, "Mr. Bowen fell in at once with me and commenced talking about Mr. Tilton, and not favorably." The publisher told him of at least three specific adulteries Tilton had been guilty of, said the pastor. "I was astonished," he was to say in court, "as you well might think, but not so much so as I should have been if I had not seen Bessie Turner," Mrs. Morse's emissary. Beecher then told Bowen everything that Bessie had told him previously. Bowen nodded along. "It was all, or mostly all, new to me," he later said. When he explained to Beecher why he had just demoted Tilton from editor to contributor on the *Independent*, it was Beecher's turn to nod. "It was my judgment that a man that was tainted as Mr. Tilton was could not properly be retained on such a paper as that without doing it damage," he explained. He went even further, with respect to Tilton's continued employment on the *Union*. "I thought that as the editor of the Republican organ in Brooklyn, he would be found to be a man that would get the paper into trouble," he said.

The next day, on Beecher's suggestion, Bowen talked to Mrs. Beecher; Beecher had told him she knew more about the painful subject of Tilton's derelictions than he did. The same afternoon, Tilton sat miserably at home, pondering the blunder he had made. On the advice both of his wife and of Frank Moulton, he determined he would meet Beecher "face to face." He sent a note around to Henry Bowen's office about his decision, "which I supposed would gratify him," and a short time later went to his own office. To Tilton's astonishment, "he came into my editorial chamber, and with a look of desperation on his countenance such as I had never seen there before . . . his face white as a wall . . . and with an anger and passion to which I had never dreamed him liable, and with the manner more of an insane than of a rational man, began to threaten me that, if in any interview I might have with Mr. Beecher, either then or at any other time, I should divulge to Mr. Beecher what he (Bowen) had said against him, or that he (Bowen) had had any hand in the letter requiring Mr. Beecher to vacate his pulpit, I would be cashiered from the *Independent* and the *Union*, and that the police should be called to cast me into the streets." Tilton, angered in return, said he would "not be deterred" and would say exactly what he wished to Beecher.

Now Tilton blamed Beecher for having poisoned the mind of his employer as well as having disrupted his home, and the fearful storm that would shake the foundations of the preacher's life and church, but would destroy both Tilton and his wife, was about to break. Frank Moulton was not in the least surprised when Tilton told him what had happened. They both agreed that, at any cost, Tilton should try to save himself, his job, and his family's name. Elizabeth Tilton, still sick and weak from the effects of her miscarriage, was in bed on Livingston Street, and her husband and Moulton held most of their conferences in her bedroom. She was filled with "profound distress" at the prospect of her headstrong mate alone trying to force the famous preacher from his pulpit, and she wanted Tilton to fetch Beecher to her bedside so the three of them could talk together. But Tilton refused to do this. He would still see Beecher alone, he said, but no more. So on December 29,

Elizabeth Tilton finally managed what she had been unable to do for months—namely, to tell Beecher that the secrecy of their intimacy was out.

She wrote the pastor a letter that amounted to a double confession and gave it to her husband, who carried it around with him until the evening of Friday the 30th, when he went over to Moulton's house on Remsen Street. He gave the original to Moulton after writing the gist of it on the back of the envelope, which he put in his pocket. Then he waited there while he sent Moulton to Plymouth Church to summon the preacher.

The weekly Friday-night prayer meeting was about to begin when Moulton walked in. Although his wife, Emma, belonged to the church, Moulton did not, and he knew Beecher only casually, having first met him a few years ago at the studio of a well-known artist where Beecher was having his portrait painted at the behest and expense of, of all people, Theodore Tilton. As the preacher now came forward, Moulton said: "Mr. Beecher, Mr. Theodore Tilton is at my house and wishes to see you."

"This is a prayer-meeting night, I cannot go to see him," Beecher replied.

"Well," Moulton said, "he wants to see you with regard to your relations with his family, and with regard to the letter he has sent you through Mr. Bowen. You better send somebody down to your prayer meeting for you."

Beecher pondered a moment and summoned a substitute from among the deacons of the church. As they walked along the Heights, Moulton told Beecher that, in Tilton's presence, Henry Bowen had charged him with numerous adulteries. Beecher was astonished. He said that Bowen, on the contrary, had made accusations against Tilton, and had just re-pledged his friendship.

"What can I do? What can I do?" Beecher asked excitedly.

"I don't know," said Moulton. "I am not a Christian. I am a heathen, but I will try to show you how well a heathen can serve you. I will try to help you."

They continued in silence. Sleet had begun to fall, and Beecher muttered: "This is a terrible night, there is an appropriateness in this storm." Moulton made no reply.

When they reached his house, he conducted Beecher to the second-floor front room, where Tilton was waiting. "I have brought Mr. Beecher at your request," he said. Then he bowed and retired to his parlor.

CHAPTER VI

Neither Tilton nor Beecher said hello. Tilton was standing stiffly on the far side of the room. When the preacher crossed over and sat in an easy chair indicated to him, Tilton walked silently to the door, locked it, and put the key in his pocket. Then he took a seat directly opposite Beecher.

"I presume, sir," he began, "that you received from me a few days ago, through Mr. Bowen, a letter demanding your retirement from your pulpit and from the City of Brooklyn."

"Yes, I have received it," Beecher said.

Tilton paused. "I have called you here tonight in order to say to you that you may consider that letter unwritten, unsent, blotted out—no longer in existence."

Beecher bowed his head and murmured his thanks.

"Your thanks should not go to me, but to Elizabeth," Tilton continued. "It is in her behalf that I hold this interview, and whatever I say here or in consequence of this meeting is not for your sake, not for my sake, but for her sake."

Tilton thereupon put his hand in his pocket for the envelope on the back of which he had made shorthand notes of what his wife had told him. "I will read to you a statement which Elizabeth has made," he said. "Mr. Moulton has the original. I will read to you the copy."

Beecher looked up. "Before reading that, Theodore, I wish you would tell me what Mr. Bowen has been saying against me."

Tilton replied that he was not interested in talking about Bowen. He suggested the preacher go see Bowen himself. But he quoted Bowen indirectly as having said about Beecher that "You have been guilty of adulteries with numerous members of your congregation ever since your Indianapolis pastorate, all down through these twenty-five years, that you are not a safe man to dwell in a Christian community." And he quoted Elizabeth: "She said to me, 'If Mr. Bowen makes war upon Mr. Beecher, and if you join in it, and if Mr. Beecher retires from his pulpit, as he must under such an attack, everybody will sooner or later know the reason why, and that will be to my shame and to the children's shame, and I cannot endure it.'"

Tilton now returned to the notes in his hand. The separate versions later given by him and by Beecher of what was hereupon said, the scope and extent of Tilton's first formal accusation against the minister, were to become basic to the case. As he read aloud from what he had jotted on the back of the envelope, Tilton, in his nervousness, picked it to pieces; since Elizabeth eventually burned the original when Moulton finally returned it to her, a true copy never emerged. In view of the consequent conspiracy among both Tiltons, Beecher, Moulton, and others to diminish the charge and quash the scandal, a conspiracy that at length broke down when Tilton lost patience and was led openly to seek justice and revenge against Beecher in court, the time and place and exact nature of Tilton's initial assault were to be very important. And as Elizabeth Tilton was never to testify in court, the varying accounts the two men eventually gave of what was said this stormy Friday evening posed the substantive issue on which the trial was to hang— whether it could be proved that Beecher and Elizabeth Tilton had committed adultery, or whether nothing more could be shown, under the law, than that he had perhaps inflamed her inordinate affection for him.

What Tilton testified his wife had told him back in July has already been quoted. Beecher's somewhat different version of what Tilton charged him with in this upstairs room at Moulton's house was:

> . . . that I had not only injured him in his business relations and prospects, but that I had also insinuated myself into his family and . . . in a sense superseded him there, so that in matters of religious doctrine, and in matters of the bringing up of his children, and of the household, his wife looked to me rather than to him; that I had caused her to transfer her affections from him to me in an inordinate measure . . . that I had corrupted Elizabeth, teaching her to lie, to deceive him, and hide under fair appearances her friendship to me . . . that I had tied the knot in the sanctuary of God by which they were to be bound together in an inseparable love [and] had also reached out my hand to untie that knot . . . that I had made overtures to her of an improper character.

When Tilton had finished his recitation, he recounted, "Mr. Beecher sat in his chair, and I thought he was about to speak. I waited a moment. His face and his head and his neck were blood-red, and I feared there would be some accident to him. He burst out with these words: 'Theodore, I am in a dream, this is Dante's Inferno.'" Beecher denied this. "I had listened with some contempt under the impression he was trying to bully me," he said; but he admitted that the news of Lib Tilton's confession to her husband "fell like a thunder bolt on me."

Tilton was to claim that Beecher asked for permission to visit Mrs. Tilton "for the last time." Beecher, on the other hand, insisted that Tilton was the one who suggested he see Elizabeth and verify the statements she had made. In either event, Beecher got up to go. Tilton gave him a final admonition. "See to it, sir, that you do not chide her for the confession which she has made," he said. "If you smite her with a word, I will smite you in ten-fold degree."

"This is all a wild whirl," Beecher murmured, and left the room. Tilton said the preacher went down the stairs "with his hand on the rail, staggering, and I thought he was about to fall." At the foot of the stairs Frank Moulton was waiting. All that Beecher would later say was that he felt himself "in a divided and perplexed state of mind." Moulton swore that the preacher was far more expressive. He was to quote Beecher as saying: "This comes upon me as if struck by lightning. This will kill me."

The strange role played by Frank Moulton, who became famous as "The Mutual Friend" in the Beecher-Tilton case, was prompted by his conviction that if the truth in the scandal should be made public, "a great national calamity would ensue" which "would tend to undermine the very foundations of social order, lay low a beneficent power for good in our country, and blast the prospects and blight the family of one of our most brilliant and promising of the rising men of the generation." To avoid this, and to avoid having "innocent children burdened with obloquy," Moulton, with the help of his wife, was to labor diligently for four years in a vain effort to save both Beecher and Tilton "from the consequences of their acts, whether of unwisdom or passion." While pro-Beecherites were to accuse him of conspiring with Tilton against Beecher, and even of blackmail—a charge that ultimately embarrassed Beecher far more than it helped him—Moulton did not allow his longer-standing friendship with Tilton to interfere with his earnest befriending of Beecher in need, a fact the pastor often gratefully acknowledged, with fervent thanks to God.

Moulton had been a classmate of Tilton's at the Free Academy. He had received an appointment for West Point but had declined because of bad health, and upon the recommendation of Peter Cooper he had joined Woodruff & Robinson, a prosperous mercantile house, of which he became a partner. In his early thirties, Moulton was already a highly successful businessman. His marriage to the niece of Jeremiah Robinson had not hurt his fortunes. Of medium height and rather slight, he favored a heavy mustache of the Lord Kitchener type, which made him look older than he was. He moved gracefully and with assurance, and as one of his detractors put it, "In manners he impresses one as a gentleman of refinement, with just enough of the way of the world in his make-up to preclude the idea of effeminacy." If Moulton came initially to Beecher in behalf of Tilton, it was the preacher who soon cultivated him, and who came to depend upon him even more than Tilton did. Beecher needed someone to whom he could entrust the many letters that were written in the case, which he could not afford to keep in his own house or even at the church for fear of the prying eyes of his wife; in addition, Moulton represented something Beecher, with his keen eye for character and personality, naturally appreciated. He stood for common sense, for practicality and reason. In fact, he stood squarely in the middle as a man between Theodore Tilton, the eager romantic, destined for emotional purgatory during these changing times, his wild notions always tempered by guilt, and Henry Ward Beecher, who wisely knew what was happening to the old religions and the old moral structure and who was doing his best to blow with the wind.

Both the Moultons matched candor with calmness. He as a non-believer, she as a churchgoer and a particular admirer of Beecher's, shared a sense of respectability which was as sincere as it was unpretentious. Perhaps more than any other figures in the great scandal, the Moultons showed themselves to be "ahead of the times" by their honest if painful insistence that Beecher was to be condemned more for having violated the ninth than the seventh commandment. When, for his own ends and for those of his adulators, the preacher would obtain two satisfactory if foreordained exculpations in the church that he dominated, it was the Moultons who would stand most stubbornly at his ear and, like gnats of conscience, remind him that he, a supposed paragon, had heaped worse coals upon the fires of his venal sin by cloaking it hypocritically in divine garb. Eventually, in view of Beecher's standing as one of the best-known men in America, this less exalted lapse of having tried to hide what he had done would most sorely injure the average man's pride.

When Beecher reached the foot of the stairs, whether or not he cried out that Theodore Tilton's "thunderbolt" of accusation would kill him, he asked Moulton to accompany him to the Tilton home on Livingston Street. The storm outside had begun to break. "I went forth like a sleepwalker, while clouds were flying in the sky," Beecher said. "The winds were out and whistling through the leafless trees, but all this was peace compared to my mood within."

In front of Tilton's house Moulton turned about. The Tiltons' housekeeper let Beecher in, and he went up straightway to Elizabeth's room. "Mrs. Tilton lay upon her bed, white as marble, with closed eyes, as in a trance, and with her hands upon her bosom, palm to palm, as one in prayer," he remembered. The marblelike form reminded him of some statuary he had seen in Europe. Beecher drew a chair to her bedside. When he told the story in court, he wept, as he often did when aroused.

> I said to her: "Elizabeth, I have just seen your husband . . . He has been making many statements to me, and charges, and he has sent me to you in respect to some of them, that you should verify them." I then said: "He has charged me that I have corrupted your affections from him. He has charged me that I have corrupted your simplicity and your truthfulness. He has also charged me with attempting improprieties . . . Are these things so, Elizabeth?" She—there was the faintest quiver, and tears trickled down her cheek, but no answer . . . And she opened her eyes and said: "My friend, I could not help it." "Could not help it, Elizabeth! Why could you not help it? You know that these things are not true." "Oh, Mr. Beecher," said she, "I was wearied out . . . He made me think that if I would confess love to you, it would help him confess his alien affections," or words to that effect. "But," I said to her, "Elizabeth, this is a charge of attempting improper

things. You know that is not true." "Yes, it is not true," she says, "but what can I do?" "Do! You can take it back again." She hesitated, and I did not understand her hesitation. "Why can you not take it back? It is not true." She said something about she would be willing to do it if it could be done without injury to her husband, which I did not at all understand. "But," I said, "you ought to give me a written retraction of that written charge."

Elizabeth "raised herself," according to Beecher, "and beckoned for her writing materials, which I handed her from her secretary standing near by." Without any help from him, he swore, she wrote the following note, which she always described as having been "dictated":

Wearied with importunities, and weakened by sickness, I gave a letter inculpating my friend. Henry Ward Beecher, under assurances that that would remove all

ELIZABETH TILTON! "I DID, I DID NOT, I DID . . ."

difficulties between me and my husband. That letter I now revoke. I was persuaded to do it, almost forced, when I was in a weakened state of mind. I regret it and recall its statements.

E. R. T.

Beecher re-read it slowly. "It seemed to me as if she was going to die, that her mind was overthrown and that I was in some dreadful way mixed up in it, and might be left by her death with this terrible accusation hanging over me," he later said. It was surely one of the most revealing understatements he ever made. But he promised Elizabeth, thereby bringing full circle the noble pledges of the principals to protect one other: "I shall not use it [the note] to the injury of your husband."

It was almost ten o'clock when the pastor left and went back to Frank Moulton's place. As Moulton then walked him home, Beecher said nothing of the retraction in his pocket. "He said he wanted me to be a friend to him in this terrible business," was all that Moulton recalled.

It was after midnight when Theodore Tilton reached home. Lucy Mitchell, the nurse who was taking care of Mrs. Tilton, was sleeping alongside her when a "buzzing sound" awakened her. It was Tilton, talking to his wife. He ordered the nurse out of the room, despite her protestations that "this will never do, Mrs. Tilton must not be disturbed so." From the next room, Mrs. Mitchell heard Tilton shouting and Mrs. Tilton "in a tone of entreaty." Elizabeth, according to Tilton, "said that Mr. Beecher had been there, telling her that she had pursued and slain him." He had been so aroused that she had been afraid he might kill her, Tilton claimed she added. Fetching pen and ink, he gave them to his wife, who never denied that she wrote the following voluntarily:

December 30, 1870—Midnight

MY DEAR HUSBAND: I desire to leave with you before going to sleep a statement that Mr. Henry Ward Beecher called upon me this evening, asked me if I would defend him against any accusation in a *council of ministers*, and I replied solemnly that I would in case the accuser was any other but my husband. He (H. W. B.) dictated a letter, which I copied as my own, to be used by him against any other accuser except my husband. This letter was designed to vindicate Mr. Beecher against all other persons save only yourself. I was ready to give him this letter because he said with pain that my letter in your hands addressed to him, dated December 29, "had struck him dead and ended his usefulness." You and I both are pledged to do our best to avoid publicity. God grant a speedy end to all further anxieties. Affectionately,

Elizabeth

When Nurse Mitchell was permitted by Tilton to return to Mrs. Tilton's side, she found her "agitated" and "stroked her head and tried to pacify her." Over on Columbia Heights, Beecher was already asleep. In another masterful understatement he was to say: "I felt there was more to come than I knew that night." But no matter what his troubles, nor even his prescience of trouble, the preacher always slept soundly, ten hours' worth if he could.

CHAPTER VII

The morning after the multiple events of December 30, Elizabeth Tilton called Frank Moulton to her sickbed. She was more distraught than ever, and very pale. She begged him, both orally and in writing, to try to get back from Beecher the note she had written at the pastor's dictation. She told Moulton she wanted to burn it, along with her confession.

That evening, after supper, Moulton went around to Beecher's house on Columbia Heights. He had in his jacket a small pistol he always carried because of his frequent business tours around the rough area of the New York docks. Beecher greeted him at the door, and the two men adjourned to a second-floor bedroom. There Moulton related the substance of what Mrs. Tilton had written her husband at midnight, after Beecher had left with the retraction of her confession in his pocket. The pastor at first was silent, but he finally said he was "surprised."

Moulton regarded him carefully. "Mr. Beecher," he said, measuredly, "I think you have been guilty of a great meanness in getting the permission of a husband to visit his house and then going there to his wife and procuring from her what you know to be a lie. That won't save you. I did not see . . . much of the guidance of God in what you did. . ."

When Moulton asked for the return of the retraction, promising either to burn it himself with Mrs. Tilton's confession or save both, Beecher protested that he needed the note in case Tilton brought formal charges against him. "In case of my death," he declared, "this would be the only defense that my family would have."

"Mr. Beecher, I do not think that you now ought to take merely selfish counsel of yourself," Moulton persisted. "The truth is the truth. You have got to abide by that. Where is the retraction? I want it."

Beecher stood up and hesitated. Then he walked slowly to the bureau in the corner and took Elizabeth Tilton's letter from a drawer. He walked back equally slowly and handed it to Moulton. As he was doing this, Moulton had begun to take his coat off—Beecher said "he had been sweating"—and the pastor noticed the hilt of the gun sticking out. Moulton took the pistol from the jacket and laid it on his knee. He patted the hilt and promised Beecher he would protect the retraction note "to this extent, with my life." This became famous later as "The Pistol Incident." While Beecher's defenders were to impute the threat of force and evil intent to Moulton, Beecher himself was to swear in court, with a degree of embarrassment, that he had not observed any "intimidation or coercion" on Moulton's part.

After the display of the pistol there took place another of the vital conversations in the case. Moulton and Beecher, the only persons present, were to disagree violently when it came to be repeated. Moulton would testify that Beecher, "with great sorrow, weeping," told him "that he had loved Elizabeth Tilton very much" and that "the expression, the sexual expression of that love, was just as natural in his opinion—he had thought so—as the language that he had used to her."

Beecher was to deny vehemently that the subject of "criminal connection" between himself and Mrs. Tilton came up. "Such language is simply impossible to me," he would say of Moulton's paraphrase. He also denied saying, as Moulton swore he did, that he was "on the brink of a moral Niagara" and that "since you know the truth, I would throw myself upon your friendship, and what I believe to be your desire to save me." His voluntary surrender of the retraction letter, Beecher said, was "a work of conciliation" which he thought would help Moulton keep Tilton in check. He was never able to explain satisfactorily, however, why he so willingly gave up his sole "shield of defense," as Tilton's lawyers were to put it, to a man he scarcely knew, especially in view of his insistence that he had been wrongfully accused. The only reason he ever gave was that Moulton seemed "a very cultivated, literary man, as well as a businessman, whose wife was a member of my church, and whom I thought to be a good man, true and honorable." When the question was put, with some sarcasm: "You did not then suppose, did you, that he knew the nature of the charge against you?" Beecher weakly answered: "I don't suppose that I had any thought about that."

About the same time that Moulton was persuading Beecher to part with Elizabeth Tilton's retraction, two letters were delivered to Tilton at home from Henry Bowen, announcing his dismissal from the two editorial chairs he held, as a contributor to the *Independent* and as editor of the *Brooklyn Union*, and suggesting arbitration to determine how much severance pay was due him. Tilton told his wife about this "new surprise," and after bidding her "not to be troubled," he went to Moulton's house. Moulton, just back from Beecher's place, showed him the returned retraction, and after locking it up in a bureau with the original copy of Mrs. Tilton's confession, the two men went for a long walk. It was New Year's Eve, and Tilton later said they walked "the wintry streets till the chimes rang out the old and rang in the new year." The next morning Tilton wrote a long letter to Bowen in which he reminded the publisher of the many times he had heard Bowen allude to various adulteries of Henry Ward Beecher, and expressing "surprise and regret" at the about-face which had now become involved with his own dismissal. Tilton designated Moulton to act for him on a contract settlement. Late that afternoon, for the first time in many years, Bowen attended the annual New Year's Day reception at the Beechers', and when he whispered to Beecher that he had fired Tilton, the preacher murmured his approval.

The next afternoon, on Beecher's invitation, Moulton went to the preacher's house again. He told Beecher that the charges of loose moral conduct against Tilton which Beecher had heard from Bowen and Mrs. Morse, Tilton's ever talkative mother-in-law, were false. "Mr. Moulton told me that, of his own personal knowledge . . . he believed Mr. Tilton to be a man absolutely chaste and faithful," Beecher was to say. He told Moulton in reply that "if there was anything in this earth that I abhorred, it was scandal, and talking and rumors about people, that I had kept myself clean from them . . . and to find myself caught in the slum of them myself was very hard for my pride." Beecher added that "I was ashamed and mortified" for having believed the gossip, "and that it was all the worse because it was toward a friend whom I had known and whom I had loved, and whose household was to me like my own home, and that it was not the way Mr. Tilton had treated me when I was in adversity." Moulton would go further, saying the pastor wept "in misery" for the crime he had committed against the Tiltons, especially as brought home by the impact of Bowen's firing of Tilton and the "piteous" effect it had on Tilton's "little children."

Beecher walked up and down the room "in great agitation and self-condemnation," as he put it. His subsequent testimony, a weepy *mea culpa*, was to convince millions of his great goodness in being able to admit a wrong; the fact that after this admission he could be further accused of a carnal sin infuriated those who admired and loved him. What counted was the process of confession, not the substance. He said, as usual, that he was bewildered by what had apparently taken place, "but it seemed to me that if she had been led to transfer her affections from her husband by reason of my presence I could not but feel that I was blameworthy; that she was a woman so quiet and so simple, her exterior life was so far from that, that I had never suspected it, but that her conduct seemed to be now such as led me to feel that . . . I had warped her affections . . . It seemed to me that she must have been broken down in her moral nature . . . that great mischief had been done in that household, and that I had been the occasion of it was very plain and very evident."

When Moulton told him that Elizabeth Tilton "loves your little finger more than she does Mr. Tilton's whole body"—a statement Moulton denied making—Beecher said he accepted the condition. "I had no means of contradiction," he added. "I said to myself, 'It has been a smoldering fire, burning, concealed, and I knew nothing of it.' I felt the impulse, I suppose, which every gentleman will understand, to say 'I ought to have foreseen. I was the oldest man, the oldest person. I was the one that had the experience; she was a child. If she did not know that the tendrils of her affection were creeping up upon me, I ought to have known it.'"

THE FAMOUS "APOLOGY"

Scene in Beecher's parlor as the preacher, on a couch, discusses with Frank Moulton how to word his apology to Theodore Tilton.

Ultimately, Beecher would go much further in moving from sympathy and dismay to anger and denunciation of Lib Tilton, but at the moment he described he was deeply remorseful. "I thought it was my duty to retrace my steps and apologize, or to do anything I could to repair the mischief," was his conclusion.

Moulton listened patiently to the preacher's grandiloquent self-condemnation, and then suggested Beecher write to Tilton and "express to him the grief you feel, and the contrition for it," adding he thought Tilton "would be satisfied with that." Beecher again was "in a whirl" and asked Moulton to take pen and paper. He thereupon "dictated," Moulton said, what became known in the case as "The Letter of Contrition." Beecher denied the dictation, claiming he walked back and forth and kept talking while Moulton made notes, and that the language was Moulton's, not his. As published:

In trust with F. D. Moulton

it said on top, and then:

My dear friend Moulton:
I ask through you Theodore Tilton's forgiveness, and I humble myself before him as I do before my God. He would have been a better man in my circumstances than I have been. I can ask nothing except that he will remember all the other hearts that would ache. I will not plead for myself; I even wish that I were dead. But others must live and suffer. I will die before anyone but myself shall be inculpated. All my thoughts are running toward my friends, toward the poor child lying there and praying with her folded hands. She is guiltless, sinned against, bearing the transgressions of another. Her forgiveness I have. I humbly pray to God that He may put it in the heart of her husband to forgive me. I have trusted this to Moulton in confidence.

H. W. Beecher

It was five o'clock, and the supper bell was ringing, so Beecher hastily wrote his name "on the edge of the paper, and remote as nearly as I could from the text," meaning, he later insisted, only to give approval to the final line.

The writing of this letter became the most debated episode in the Beecher-Tilton case, and what the letter said was no more significant than what it failed to say in the light of Beecher's ultimate public defense of himself—that Mrs. Tilton had told a falsehood about his improper advances and that Tilton had made the mistake of believing her. If this was so, Beecher was never able to explain why he did not categorically deny the untruth in the apology. "I thought I was doing it," he later said, but when the letter was re-read to him and he was asked where it showed any denial of guilt, he altered course again and replied: "That is not my document," though he agreed it expressed correctly his "sentiments." The Moultons were to swear that from this moment on, in private conversation with them, Beecher never sought to deny his intimacy with Elizabeth Tilton. It was Beecher himself, for example, they insisted, who told them he had "prayed to God" with Mrs. Tilton during the summer of 1870 "for help to discontinue our sexual relations." Beecher's response to this in court was typical: "Pooh! No, sir," he said—adding that Mrs. Tilton had been suffering from "depression and mental trouble, and I prayed with her as I would with any other parishioner."

It was a fact that the penitence of the preacher was quickly pressed. On January 2, the day after he had given Moulton "The Letter of Contrition" to show to Tilton, Beecher wrote to Henry Bowen that "I have reason to think that the only cases of which I spoke to you in regard to Mr. Tilton were exaggerated in being reported to me." But he made no suggestion that Tilton be reinstated in one or both of his jobs. Bowen was scarcely impressed. "I read the letter and laid it aside," he recalled.

The following day Beecher and Tilton met again, unexpectedly, at Moulton's. Tilton refused even to greet the minister, and Moulton rebuked him for "such absolute discourtesy."

THE UNEXPECTED MEETING AT MOULTON'S
Tilton, standing in front of Moulton's sick bed, reluctantly greets Beecher.

"How can you expect me to speak to a man who has ruined my wife and broken my home?" Tilton asked.

Moulton replied that Beecher had, in his opinion, "done everything a man could do, up to the point of making a public statement of the facts." He added: "You should at least greet him civilly."

The preacher then turned to Tilton. "Theodore, I hope that my expression toward you in my letter you will feel to be a sincere one," he said. "I will do anything in my power consistent with truth and honor to make reparation for the wrong I have done you."

"That is an apology, Theodore, which any gentleman ought to accept," Moulton interjected.

Tilton finally murmured "Good morning," and he and Beecher shook hands. Beecher then repeated, verbally, the gist of his written apology, declaring he was filled with "profound sorrow" for having hurt Tilton in his job and "unconsciously and unintentionally done injury" to his wife by failing to realize that his pastoral attentions had created in her an "overweening affection" for him. Tilton said that Beecher "wept again and again, and his face assumed a very peculiar redness," that he offered to resign, to bow his head "and go out of public life," and that he begged that the facts of his adultery be kept from the ears of Mrs. Beecher. Tilton said the preacher again insisted his sexual commerce with Mrs. Tilton had come "through love and not through lust," that he had sought "companionship in her mind," as shown by the fact that he had brought her his manuscripts to read. Tilton quoted Beecher as finally having asked: "I have this request to make—that if it be necessary for you to make public a recital of this case, you will give me notice in advance of your intention to do so in order that I may either go out of the world by suicide, or else escape from the face of my friends by a voyage to some foreign land." Beecher was to deny with his usual vehemence these additional statements, calling them "intolerable" and "odiously false." Both Moulton and Mrs. Moulton, however, let alone Tilton, in time quoted him as repeating the same thoughts and avowals in varying fashion.

Beecher began seeing Moulton almost constantly, sometimes at his own house but usually over on Remsen Street, where there would be less chance of arousing the suspicions of Eunice Beecher. Under the generalship of "The Mutual Friend," whom he once jokingly addressed as "My Dear Von Moltke," the conscience-stricken pastor supported new efforts to reestablish Tilton professionally. Moulton and his business partners, who had come to know something of the case, subscribed more than $10,000 to back a new weekly called the *Golden Age* for Tilton to edit, and Beecher also helped, eventually mortgaging his house to keep the paper afloat with a gift of $5,000.

It was agreed all around that the removal from the scene of Bessie Turner, the Tiltons' adopted daughter whom Mrs. Morse had used to spread her gossip, would help matters; so Bessie was packed off to a boarding school in Ohio, with Beecher paying a large part of the expenses. Before she left, she acceded to Mrs. Tilton's request to help Tilton by writing two expedient letters. In one she denied, as she had previously charged, that Tilton had made overtures to her. She wrote:

My Dear Mrs. Tilton:

The story that Mr. Tilton once lifted me from my bed and carried me screaming to his room and attempted to violate my person is a wicked lie.

Yours truly, Bessie

In court, Bessie was to make the further explanation that Tilton "carried me from my bed, but he never carried me *screaming*." She was "perfectly unconscious" when this occurred, she added. Bessie also admitted she had been reluctant to put her name to the letter. She quoted Mrs. Tilton, who had written it for her, as saying: "Do it for me, darling, it will help Theodore."

Bessie's other letter was even more to the point. In it she told Mrs. Tilton :

. . . Your mother, Mrs. Morse, has repeatedly attempted to hire me, by offering me dresses and presents, to go to certain persons and tell them *stories* injurious to the character of your husband. I have been persuaded that the kind attentions shown me by Mr. Tilton for years were dishonorable demonstrations. I never at the time thought that Mr. Tilton's caresses were for such a purpose. I do not want to be made use of by Mrs. Morse or any one else to bring trouble on my two best friends, you and your husband.

Bye by,
Bessie Turner

This one, as it turned out, was suggested and dictated by Tilton, in a conversation he and Bessie had. In court, Bessie demonstrated a superb naïveté or her own peculiar brand of rationalization when she came to testify on the subject. She quoted herself as having told Tilton: "No, sir, she [Mrs. Morse] did not bribe me, but she said if I would go around and tell this to Mr. Beecher"—the tales of Tilton's bad treatment of his wife—"she would give me something nice." Bessie did not deny that the letter properly described what Mrs. Morse had done; but the fact that she stuck to her story of Tilton's advances, whether they were "dishonorable" or, as she finally called them, simply "immodest," was enough, as far as many were concerned, to leave Tilton still blacker than Beecher.

It was not so easy for Moulton and the others now trying desperately to quash the scandal to handle the erratic Mrs. Morse, who figured she had come to have a proprietary interest in Beecher. Toward the end of January 1871 she wrote the preacher a long, rambling letter in which she accused Tilton of "leaving my sick and distracted child to care for all four children night and day, without fire in the furnace or anything like comfort or nourishment in the house." Tilton, she said, had already told twelve persons about the scandal, a fact that even if true would scarcely have excused Mrs. Morse's own original and costly tattling. Beecher had said something to Mrs. Morse, at the time when he and his wife had counseled a separation for the Tiltons, about Mrs. Beecher "adopting" Elizabeth. Now Mrs. Morse berated Beecher for doing nothing to help Mrs. Tilton. "You or anyone else who advises her to live with him [Tilton], when he is doing all he can to kill her by slow torture, is anything but a friend," she wrote angrily. "Do you know when I hear of your cracking your jokes from Sunday to Sunday, and think of the misery you have brought upon us, I think with the Psalmist, 'There is no God.'" Beecher showed the letter to Moulton and to Tilton, and after a council of war the preacher wrote a careful reply, saying he sympathized with her "distress" but advising her that "the greatest kindness to you and to all will be . . . to leave to time the rectification of all wrongs, whether they be real or imaginary."

Mrs. Morse vented her spleen against Tilton in various ways. In addition to sending him vituperative notes, even though she was seeing him most of the time, she mailed a letter to Bowen, signed "Subscriber," which indicated her true feelings about Tilton's dismissal. "I congratulate you upon being rid of an Infidel, Liar, Hypocrite, Unbeliever, Free-Lover, a Tyrant, Knave and FOOL," she told the publisher. Bowen, virtually the only figure in the great scandal who was wise enough not to keep writing letters, did not answer this one either. But about the same time he ran into Mrs. Morse's ally, Mrs. Beecher, on the train one morning, en route to Connecticut. They did not speak, but Bowen subsequently observed that "My sullen neighbor keeps the dark and lurid past vividly before my mind. There is a look of desperation in her eye, as if she were competent to do anything bitter or revengeful."

Beecher was getting letters from others too. His brother-in-law, F. B. Perkins, wrote to him, having heard the scandal rumors and wanting to know what they were all about. Beecher reassured him. "If my friends put their foot silently on any coals or hot embers and crush them out *without talking*, the miserable lies will be as dead in New York in a little time as they are in Brooklyn," he replied. "If the papers do not meddle, this slander will fall still-born, dead as Julius Caesar."

Aided by Moulton, the two principles, Beecher and Tilton, drew closer. Moulton almost died of rheumatic fever in the winter of 1871, and Beecher was filled with sorrow, and perhaps with fear, over the possible loss of the valuable "mutual friend." The preacher met Tilton once again in Moulton's parlor and, according to Tilton, in a sudden gesture put both hands on Tilton's face and kissed him on the forehead. "He is right by four inches, I kissed him on his mouth," Beecher later amplified it.

There were two other meetings, both at Tilton's house, at one of which Beecher later said he restated the case for their revived friendship and sat on Tilton's knee "to make the appeal closer." Mrs. Tilton entered and "burst out laughing" and then "kissed me very cordially." The second meeting took place in Mrs. Tilton's bedroom, Beecher said, and "I kissed him and he kissed me, and I kissed his wife and she kissed me, and I believe they kissed each other."

Tilton indicated it was not solely a kissing-bee. Mrs. Tilton had already written her letter to a friend referring to the miscarriage she had just suffered as "a love-babe," which, as Moulton later pointed out, "is a very curious expression from a woman nearly forty years old and the mother of six children (two had died) to describe a child begotten in lawful wedlock, especially when, as Mrs. Tilton asserts, she and her husband had been fiercely quarreling for many months." Now Tilton was even more worried about some earlier conceptions. He said he had summoned Beecher and informed him: "I have called you, sir, in order that you may remove, if you can, a shadow from the future life of the little boy, Ralph," who was then two years old. "His mother has assigned to me a date at which your criminal intimacy with her began." According to Tilton, Beecher swore that the date Elizabeth had given, October 10, 1868, was correct, making him feel much better about Ralph's paternity. Beecher later swore this conversation was "a monstrous and absolute falsehood."

The orgy of letter-writing continued. Beecher wanted to be "satisfied of Theodore's spirit" toward him, and he wanted permission to write to Mrs. Tilton again. So under the same

"WHEN SHALL WE THREE MEET AGAIN?"

date, three letters were duly penned. Tilton wrote to Moulton that "notwithstanding the great suffering which he [Beecher] has caused to Elizabeth and myself, I bear him no malice, shall do him no wrong, shall discountenance every project by whomsoever proposed for any exposure of his secret to the public." Beecher wrote to Moulton that "Many, many friends has God raised up to me, but to no one of them has He ever given the opportunity and the wisdom to serve me as you have. My trust in you is implicit . . . Would to God, Who orders all hearts, that by your kind mediation, Theodore, Elizabeth and I could be made friends again. Theodore will have the hardest task in such a case; but has he not proved himself capable of the noblest things?" The pastor concluded by saying that his most earnest longing was to see Mrs. Tilton "in the full sympathy of her nature at rest in him," her husband, "to see him once more trusting her, and loving her with even a better than the old love." He was both pessimistic and hopeful. "Is there a way out of this night?" he asked. "May not a day star arise?"

And Beecher also wrote to Elizabeth. "When I last saw you," he told her, "I did not expect ever to see you again or to be alive many days. God was kinder to me than were my own thoughts." He praised Moulton's hand "that tied up the storm that was ready to burst upon our head" and that "In him we have common ground." The past, said the preacher, was ended, but Moulton might remain "a priest in the new sanctuary of reconciliation." It was Tilton who carried this letter to Elizabeth on her sickbed; he then gave it to Moulton, who put all three of them in his padlocked bureau drawer.

Not all the writing was so open. Although Beecher and Mrs. Tilton were not supposed to communicate with each other, they violated this pledge by the exchange of what came to be known in the case as "The Clandestine Letters." In one of these, in the spring of 1871, Lib Tilton, begging the preacher to forgive her for the trouble she had brought him, harked back to Beecher's novel, *Norwood*, and to the image of "nest-hiding" contained in one of the chapters he had read aloud to her. She wrote him:

My future either for life or death would be happier could I but feel you forgave me while you forget me. In all the sad complications of the past years, my endeavor was entirely to keep you from all suffering, to bear myself alone, leaving you forever ignorant of it. My weapons were love, a large untiring generosity, and *nest-hiding*!

Beecher was to have a hard time explaining the phrase. And then, Mrs. Tilton wrote to her pastor again:

My Dear Friend: Does your heart bound *towards all* as it should: So does mine! I am myself again. I did not dare tell you until I was sure; but the bird has sung in my heart these *four* weeks, and he has covenanted with me never again to leave . . . Of course I should like to share with you my joy, but I can wait for the Beyond! . . .

When Mrs. Beecher went South, Beecher replied:

The blessing of God rests upon you. Every spark of life and warmth of your own house will be a star and sun in my dwelling. Your note broke like spring upon winter, and gave me an inward rebound to life. No one can ever know, none but God, through what a dreary wilderness I have passed . . . If only it might lead to the Promised Land—or, like Moses, shall I die on the border? Your hope and courage are like medicine to me . . . If it would be of comfort to *you*, now and then, to send me a letter of true *inwardness*—the outcome of your inner life—it would be safe, for I am now at home here with my sister, and it is *permitted to you* . . .

During the late spring and summer, when she went away as usual, Mrs. Tilton also wrote her husband. She was reading another novel of Charles Reade's, *Griffith Gaunt*, and was much impressed by the manner in which the heroine, Catherine Gaunt, had restrained herself after conceiving a passion for

Brother Leonard, a priest. It provided Lib Tilton with a kind of revelation. "My Dear Theodore," she wrote, from Schoharie:

> Today, through the ministry of Catherine Gaunt, a character of fiction, my eyes have been opened for the first time in my experience, so that I see clearly my sin! It was when I knew that I was loved to suffer it to grow to a passion. A virtuous woman should check instantly an absorbing love. But it appeared to me in such a false light. That the love I felt and received could harm no one, not even you, I have believed unfalteringly until four o'clock this afternoon, when the heavenly vision dawned upon me. I see now, as never before, the wrong I have done you, and hasten immediately to ask your pardon, with a penitence so sincere that henceforth (if reason remains) you may trust me implicitly. Oh! my dear Theo., though your opinions are not restful or congenial to my soul, yet my own integrity and purity are a sacred and a holy thing to me. Bless God, with me, for Catherine Gaunt, and for all the sure leadings of an all-wise and loving Providence. Yes; now I feel quite prepared to renew my marriage vow to you, to keep it as the Saviour requireth, who looketh at the eye and the heart. Never before could I say this. I know not that you are yet able, or ever will be, to say this to *me*. Still, with what profound thankfulness that I am to come to this sure foundation, and that my feet are planted on the rock of this great truth, you cannot at all realize. When you yearn toward me with any true feeling, be assured of the tried, purified, and restored love of Elizabeth.

It was not exactly another confession, but it came pretty close to it. A week later, still in the same vein, Elizabeth wrote: "O, my dear husband, may you never need the discipline of being misled by a good woman, as I was by a good man."

Tilton could not get himself to be as forgiving as his wife wished him to be. As was so often the case, poetry proved an outlet for him, and he penned what he admitted were some biographical verses to express, "in the form of a soliloquy, the grief and sorrows of a man utterly broken down in every one of the points in which a successful life might have continued as a success." He wrote them one day on a train while riding to keep a lecture date, and he called them "Sir Marmaduke's Musings" when he printed them in the *Golden Age*:

I won a noble fame,
But with a sudden frown,
The people snatched my crown,
And in the mire trod down
My lofty name.

I bore a bounteous purse,
And beggars by the way
Then blessed me day by day
But I, grown poor as they,
Have now their curse.

I gained what men call friends,
But now their love is hate,
And I have learned, too late,
How mated minds unmate
And friendship ends.

I clasped a woman's breast,
As if her heart I knew
Or fancied would be true.
Who proved, alas! she too—
False like the rest.

I am now bereft,
As when some tower doth fall,
With battlements and wall,
And gate and bridge and all,
And nothing left.

In court Tilton was to say of his musings: "I would have cut off my right hand rather than have printed them" if "any human being would have supposed that I meant Elizabeth." But they upset everybody, Moulton as well as Elizabeth and Beecher; for in spite of the collective efforts quietly to restore old affections, the campaign to hush the affair was already being undone by the whisperings that had gone on before and were still continuing. It was inevitable, the longer and more involved the campaign, that the rumors would eventually mount to a repressed roar which, when released, would sound louder than ever across the country. There was a proper irony in the fact that it was neither Mrs. Morse nor Eunice Beecher, but the one woman no one, including Beecher and Tilton, could handle—an outsider, Victoria Woodhull—who would be responsible for blasting open the great scandal.

PART 3

THE BROKEN EGGS

CHAPTER VIII

On the morning of May 22, 1871, there appeared in the *World* a letter-to-the-editor:

> SIR: Because I am a woman, and because I conscien-
> tiously hold opinions somewhat different from the
> self-elected orthodoxy which men find their profit in
> supporting, and because I think it my bounden duty
> and my absolute right to put forward my opinions, and
> to advocate them with my whole strength, self-elected
> orthodoxy assails, vilifies me, and endeavors to cover
> my life with ridicule and dishonor . . . But let him
> that be without sin cast the stone. I do not intend to
> be made the scapegoat of sacrifice, to be offered up as
> a victim to society by those who cover over the foul-
> ness of their lives and the feculence of their thoughts
> with a hypocritical mantle of fair professions, and by
> diverting public attention from their own iniquity in
> pointing the finger at me. I know that many of my
> self-appointed judges and critics are deeply tainted
> with the vices they condemn . . . I advocate free love
> in its highest, purest sense as the only cure for the
> immorality, the deep damnation by which men cor-
> rupt and disfigure God's most holy institution of

sexual relation. My judges preach against "free love" openly, and practice it secretly; their outward seeming is fair, inwardly they are full of "dead men's bones and all manner of uncleanness." For example, I know of one man, a public teacher of eminence, who lives in concubinage with the wife of another public teacher of almost equal eminence. All three concur in denouncing offenses against morality. "Hypocrisy is the tribute paid by vice to virtue." So be it: but I decline to stand up as the "frightful example." I shall make it my business to analyze some of these lives, and will take my chances in the matter of libel suits.

I have no faith in critics, but I believe in justice.

VICTORIA C. WOODHULL

Later in the morning Mrs. Woodhull sent a message around to the office of Theodore Tilton's new magazine, the *Golden Age*, and said she wanted to see him. Tilton had never met Mrs. Woodhull, but he knew her by name, as did almost everyone in New York, as a radical spiritualist. She and her younger sister, Tennessee Claflin—she spelled it "Tennie C." and called herself a "magnetic healer"—had become famous as the "She Broker" financial wards of Commodore Vanderbilt. The Commodore had set them up in a sumptuous suite at 44 Broad Street and boasted that he got his market tips from the clairvoyant pair. He even attributed a killing in railway securities to Mrs. Woodhull's having predicted a stock rise "in a trance," but it was common gossip in Wall Street that he was the one furnishing the tips and that he was so infatuated with Tennie C. that he would have married her if his family had not intervened. Vanderbilt also was the backer of *Woodhull and Claflin's Weekly*, a sixteen- page paper with the masthead maxim "Progress! Free Thought! Untrammeled Lives!" The paper was now a year old, and with the help of a motley staff of spiritualists, itinerant philosophers, and worshipping office-boys Mrs. Woodhull was making good on her declaration: "Wherever I find a social carbuncle, I shall plunge my surgical knife of reform into it *up to the hilt!*"

THE "SHE BROKERS"
*Woodhull and Claflin, Commodore Vanderbilt's protégées,
driving the bulls and bears of Wall Street.*

As a social reformer, in her lectures as well as in her weekly, Victoria Woodhull was a passionate and unrestrained champion of action. She attacked with vengeance everything from the lack of public housing to the hypocrisy of public houses frequented by prominent "respectable" men. Less vocal and less courageous, if perhaps more sensible, reformers regarded her and her sisters as a wild, impractical pair whose advanced notions about the freedom of relations between the sexes threatened to do more harm than good to the cause of female emancipation. The fact that Mrs. Woodhull maintained a lavish but queer ménage that included her husband, Dr. Canning Woodhull, a kindly but alcoholic physician, as well as what she termed her brevet husband, a Civil War veteran named Colonel James Blood, gave her detractors enough to talk about. The easy susceptibility to masculine blandishments of Tennie C., and the raffish qualities of the rest of the family, especially the sisters' father and mother, provided further fuel.

Nevertheless, the two girls, while they were not actually beautiful, had a dash and flair that were not yet referred to as sex appeal, and their deportment was more vivacious than vulgar. Their slight, compact figures were always well-bodiced and were topped off by mannish jackets and ties; their skirts stopped daringly at their shoe-tops. They kept their hair short and curly and wore nobby Alpine hats. On a sleeve of her dresses Victoria had stitched a verse from the 120th Psalm: "Deliver my soul, O Lord, from lying lips and from a deceitful tongue." She belied her wicked reputation by a certain platform refinement and dignity, which she retained even when she grew most eloquent and vehement, which was when she was hissed. And when she cried: "I have been smeared all over with the most opprobrious epithets and the vilest names, am stigmatized as a bawd and a blackmailer, but until you are ready to suffer what I have suffered, do not dare to impugn my motives," there was a note of ringing sincerity that elicited more cheers than jeers.

Theodore Tilton's mixed feelings about Victoria Woodhull were pretty typical, until he met her. Her summons was obeyed by him as much out of curiosity as anything else. When he reached her office, she immediately handed him a copy of the

VICTORIA C. WOODHULL AND TENNIE C. CLAFLIN

World and pointed out her letter. He began reading it to himself, until she asked him to read aloud, which he did, including the part about the "public teacher" who lived "in concubinage" with another eminent man's wife.

"Do you know, sir, to whom I refer in that card?" Mrs. Woodhull asked, when he had finished.

"How can I tell to whom you refer in a blind card like this?" Tilton replied, somewhat hollowly.

"I refer, sir, to the Reverend Henry Ward Beecher and your wife," said Mrs. Woodhull.

Tilton gulped and muttered his astonishment.

Mrs. Woodhull smiled up at him winsomely. "I read, sir, by the expression on your face, that it is true," she said.

She thereupon gave what Tilton later described as "an extravagant and violent" account of his domestic troubles, including not only the substance of his wife's confession of adultery but further magnified details of how he had dragged her out to the grave of their infants, torn the wedding ring from her finger and stamped it into the cemetery ground, and of how Frank Moulton had demanded and received from Beecher some incriminating papers by threatening him with death at pistol point. There was little doubt in Tilton's mind where it had all come from—"through the open-gate lips of Mrs. Morse," his mother-in-law.

But Mrs. Morse had not been the sole source.

During the previous year Victoria Woodhull had shifted her interest from spiritualism, brokerage, and random social causes to politics and the women's movement. Her mentor was one of the leading spiritualist philosophers of the day, Stephen Pearl Andrews. This rather remarkable son of a Baptist minister had broken away from the church, become an abolitionist, studied Swedenborg and Fourier, founded a universal language—the forerunner of Esperanto, which he called Alwato—introduced phonography into the United States, written several vast and largely unread tomes that were mixtures of his considerable philosophic and linguistic knowledge (he studied many languages, among them Chinese), and, finally, become a doctor.

A quiet, dreamy, bearded man, Andrews, almost sixty, was "The Pantarch" of a scheme for world government called "The Pantarchy" when he met Victoria Woodhull, half his age. In her he at once saw his ideal instrument; her belief in the efficacy of dynamic spirits and her personal magnetism made her the perfect person to dramatize his dream of a better life.

Andrews promptly told Mrs. Woodhull that she was destined to become President of the United States. It was all she needed to hear. In April 1870 the announcement of her candidacy was made in the form of a "First Pronunciamento," which appeared in the *New York Herald.* There was nothing bashful about Victoria, especially with Andrews behind her. With a degree of truth, she declared herself to be "the most prominent representative of the only unrepresented class in the Republic . . . the most practical exponent of the principles of equality," and she pointed out that while other women leaders had engaged in crusades of talk she had "boldly entered the arena" against men and had successfully competed with them in business. "I therefore claim the right to speak for the unenfranchised women of the country," she said, "and believing as I do that the prejudices which still exist in the popular mind against women in public life will soon disappear, I now announce myself as a candidate for the Presidency . . . The platform that is to succeed in the coming election must enunciate the general principles of enlightened justice and economy. . ."

A series of papers on "The Tendencies of Government," mostly written by Andrews but revealing Mrs. Woodhull's flair for violent expression, began appearing in the *Herald.* They all bore her name, and as they covered more and more history and utopian theory, and showed signs of considerable erudition, they drew growing attention, especially among spiritualists. Spiritualism had become a fad in America, and there were several million believers of varying degrees of visionary intensity and doctrine. In their general outlook, they often seemed to agree with reformers seeking to loosen the strings of social convention. Neither the conservative spokesmen of legislative reform, such as Julia Ward Howe and her associates in the right wing of the suffragist movement, nor Susan Anthony, Elizabeth Cady Stanton, Isabella Beecher Hooker, and other ladies of the more liberal wing, particularly welcomed this "affinity" with the spiritualists. In a time of change, however, it was inevitable that those who peered into the future would get together, and Victoria Woodhull saw to it that the "affinities" touched.

With the help of another magnetic personality, Benjamin Butler, the gnome-like lawyer-abolitionist and Greenbacker, who had been dubbed "Beast Butler" when he ruled New Orleans after the Civil War with a minimum of respect for Southern chivalry, Mrs. Woodhull made a roaringly successful debut in behalf of female suffrage. She descended on Washington late in December 1870, just as the National Women's Suffrage Association, headed by Susan Anthony and Elizabeth Cady Stanton, was opening its third annual convention. But Mrs. Woodhull neatly bypassed the association. Butler had arranged for her to appear before the Judiciary Committee of the House of Representatives, the first woman ever to do so. Mrs. Woodhull wore a conservative dark dress. When she got up to speak she looked pale to the point of fainting, as she often did before making a public address, but her trembling voice soon mounted to a musical, passionate crescendo. Her memorial on woman suffrage, which Butler had written, took the whole town, and especially the ladies at the convention by storm. She had proved herself so much more effective than they were that, even though some of them were still a little hesitant about it, Victoria Woodhull over-night was made the darling of the suffragist movement. Miss Anthony, Mrs. Stanton, and Mrs. Hooker now virtually adopted Victoria. Mrs. Hooker, Beecher's half-sister, who had previously ridiculed her, introduced her at the convention the following day and soon started calling her "My Darling Queen," declaring: "That little woman has bridged with her prostrate body an awful gulf over which womanhood will walk to her freedom." Susan Anthony said: "If it takes youth, beauty and money to capture Congress, Victoria is the woman we are after." But it was Mrs. Stanton who chiefly took Victoria under her respectable and ample wing. And it was Mrs. Stanton, being only human and enjoying good gossip as much as anyone, and happening to be coincidentally annoyed at Henry Ward Beecher for his switch in allegiance to Julia Ward Howe's suffrage camp, who whispered to Mrs. Woodhull the story about the adultery of the pastor with the wife of Theodore Tilton.

What Mrs. Stanton knew was beyond the realm of gossip: she had been told the story by Tilton himself the night during the recent summer when he had poured his heart out to her and to Laura Curtis Bullard over dinner in Brooklyn, and she had been able to check it against what Elizabeth Tilton had told Susan Anthony that same night at the Tilton home. So there was no reason for Mrs. Woodhull to doubt it—not that she would have anyway. But Mrs. Stanton did not realize what ammunition she was furnishing Victoria. When she later did—when it was too late—she wrote to her friend, Miss Anthony: "Offended Susan: Come right down and pull my ears. I shall not attempt a defense. Of course I admit that I have made an awful blunder in not keeping silent as far as you were concerned on this terrible Beecher-Tilton scandal. The whole odium of this *scandalum magnatum* has been rolled on our suffrage movement. . ."

Once she had heard about it, Mrs. Woodhull lost little time in keeping the scandal ball bouncing. A few days after Mrs. Stanton had made the disclosure to her, she had a conversation, arranged by Isabella Beecher Hooker, with Henry Ward Beecher's puritanical sister Catherine. It was a signally unsuccessful session. The stern Miss Beecher, who had little use for suffragists and none for spiritualists, subsequently described her distaste: "I accepted an invitation from Victoria Woodhull to ride with her in Central Park," she wrote. "The result was an impression that she was either insane or the hapless victim of malignant spirits. For she calmly informed me that several distinguished editors, clergymen and lady authors of this city, some of them my personal friends and all of them models of domestic purity and virtue, not only held her opinions on free love, but practice accordingly; and that it was only a lack of moral courage that prevented their open avowal of such opinions. I concealed all this excepting from a few personal friends, because it is cruelty and a disgrace to any person of delicacy and refinement, especially to ladies, to have their names and character publicly subjected to injury as to such practices." Mrs. Woodhull's version was, as usual, somewhat different. After giving vent to her theories of free love, she said, she "frankly told her [Miss Beecher] what I knew about her brother, Henry Ward Beecher, and other eminent men and women . . . She took it upon herself to vouch for Mr. Beecher's faithfulness to his marriage vows, though I compelled her to admit she had no positive knowledge which could justify her in so doing." They parted uncomfortably. Mrs. Woodhull quoted Miss Beecher as saying: "'Remember, Victoria Woodhull, that I shall strike you dead.' I replied, 'Strike as much and as hard as you please, only don't do it in the dark so that I cannot know who is my enemy.'"

The trouble was, it hardly required someone as stern and unbending as Catherine Beecher to strike at Victoria Woodhull and find a mark. Even if a lot of blemishes in her past were more her family's fault than hers, Victoria had not exactly led a clean and wholesome life. It would have been impossible, under the conditions and circumstances in which she had been raised. To appreciate the position in which she now found herself, and her own brand of fury at Catherine Beecher's derogatory attitude, the strange saga of the Claflins must be considered.

They were a brawling, shiftless brood whose eccentricities were forever getting them in trouble with the law. Reuben Buckman Claflin, the father, had moved west from Massachusetts as a boy, had been a horse-trader and river gambler, and had tried almost anything for a living, including counterfeiting. He was an attractive man in a malevolent sort of way, big and bony, inspiring confidence through bluster. A fast talker, he was a pettifogger who enjoyed getting in and out of scrapes. He met Roxanna Hummel in a small Susquehanna Valley town, where she worked as a maid, and when he married her, took her out West. They finally settled in Homer, Ohio. Roxanna Claflin had ten children, not all of whom lived, and those who did received scant parental care and affection and endured in squalor and chaos in an unpainted, largely bedless frame shack on a hillside. Victoria, the seventh child, was the prettiest, a blue-eyed little brunette with a pert look and a dreamlike quality that could suddenly flare into expressive action. A biography noted that "she was marked from the womb with preternatural excitement," and that after having been conceived "during the frenzy of a Methodist revival and born in a treacherous nest of catamounts," she had "dug in the garden with the devil's foot as her spade, to hurry her up" and "had played with ghosts." At the age of eleven Victoria was already a revivalist, making dramatic speeches to other children from an Indian altar-mount and holding private séances with two infant sisters who had died. She kept seeing angels and the devil appearing before her in various guises so often that she soon established herself as a teen-age clairvoyant. All the members of the family, in fact, were spiritualists. Roxanna Claflin used to go out into orchards at sundown and beseech the Lord to forgive her neighbors' sins. That the neighbors never requested this service did not seem to make much difference. "My prayers come out crooked as a ram's horn, but they go up as straight as a shingle," Roxanna said.

With all their madness, the Claflins were serious eccentrics too, and a fiercely loyal, protective clan. They left Homer under mysterious circumstances involving the firing of Buck Claflin's mill—he was thought to have set fire to it himself, to collect the insurance—and began wandering from town to town in the Midwest, sometimes together, sometimes apart. Victoria and Tennessee, whose early satanic powers were believed to outstrip her sister's, joined in greeting the spirits at a boarding house in Mount Gilead, Ohio. It was not long after the Fox sisters had begun to put spiritualism on the map by crackling the joints of their toes to simulate otherworldly response; "Mr. Splitfoot" and his "Rochester Rappings" had made them rich as mediums. The Claflin sisters mixed Victoria's fortunetelling with Tennessee's magnetic healing, a process supposedly set in motion by a "Magnetic Life Elixir, for Beautifying the

Complexion and Cleansing the Blood." It sold for two dollars, and for another dollar Tennessee would "point out to the ladies and gentlemen their former, present and future partners, telling exactly those that are dead and living, their treatment, disposition and character in life." When required, she promised to "go into an unconscious state and travel to any part of the world . . ."

Victoria floated around with Tennessee until she married Dr. Woodhull when she was fifteen, in 1853. Dr. Woodhull was variously described as a rake and a crook as well as an alcoholic, but he was actually a rather gentle, mixed-up man who just fell in love with the little blue-eyed spirit-dealer, and kept on drinking when he couldn't keep up with her. In the biography of Victoria Woodhull which Theodore Tilton later wrote, Dr. Woodhull was pictured as having determined to marry Victoria—"my little chick," he called her—after a Fourth of July picnic they attended together. Tilton's account was somewhat prejudiced, for it came from Colonel Blood, who soon usurped Victoria's attentions. Tilton wrote of Dr. Woodhull: "This brilliant fop, tired of the demi-monde ladies whom he could purchase for his pleasure, and inspired with a sudden and romantic interest in this artless maid, said to her, 'My little puss, tell your father and mother I want you for a wife.'" The Claflins gave their approval, and Dr. Woodhull and his child bride moved first to Chicago and then to California, by which time Victoria had given birth to a little boy, who grew queer after he was dropped on his head at the age of two. They also had a daughter, named Zulu Maud. If Canning Woodhull did mistreat Victoria, as the biography claimed, she likewise led him a merry chase. In California she worked as a cigar-girl and a seamstress and then trod the boards with Anna Cogswell, the actress. One evening, "while clad in a pink silk dress and slippers, acting in the ball-room scene in the Corsican Brothers," as Tilton wrote, "suddenly a spirit voice addressed her, saying 'Victoria, come home.'" Victoria quickly went into a "clairvoyant condition" and saw her sister Tennessee waiting for her in New York. The next morning the Woodhulls boarded a steamer for the East, and when they arrived, so the story went, Victoria was proved right; her mother had ordered Tennessee "to send the spirits" to fetch Victoria.

With Tennessee, Victoria now resumed her career as a medium, while her sister kept up her activities as a healer. It soon brought them trouble. Tennessee came up with a cancer cure and launched a series of clinics. In 1864, in Ottawa, Illinois, this resulted in their having to flee the town when fifteen "patients" in her "infirmary" were found in a neglected and deplorable condition. Buck Claflin was back in the picture now too, as a sort of manager of his gifted children. The troupe, which included Tennessee's husband as well as Dr. Woodhull, continued its itinerant fortune-telling and patent-medicine selling in the west. Troubles with the law mounted, and the travelers were accused of blackmail and prostitution as well as quackery. But their fortunes somehow kept increasing. It was in St. Louis that Victoria met her true love, Colonel Blood, a powerfully constructed man with Dundreary whiskers. Blood was also a spiritualist, and when he came to visit Victoria she passed into a rapid trance and told him then and there that they were destined to live together as man and wife. They were betrothed on the spot by "the powers of the air," and while there are no records to show that their relationship was ever legally sealed, Victoria did divorce Canning Woodhull, though she felt sorry enough for him to take him back into her household subsequently.

Colonel Blood's wartime background was legitimate enough—he had five bullet holes in his body to prove it. He was also nobody's fool. A philosophical anarchist, he believed firmly in free love and fiat money; it was a great combination, and many spiritualists favored it. Victoria had already formed her own notions about free love, but Blood, even before Andrews, "philosophized" them for her and then became her willing foil. By free love, Mrs. Woodhull always insisted, she meant nothing more than honest affection honestly administered. Blood was a combination amanuensis and platform prop for her. They traveled around in a covered wagon, Victoria telling fortunes and making speeches and Blood doing the barking. When she

COLONEL JAMES BLOOD

got really wound up in a revivalist frenzy, she would point to the Colonel and shout: "There stands my lover, but when I cease to love him, I shall leave him," and when she added: "I hope, however, that time will never come," Colonel Blood managed a sickly, hirsute grin.

In 1868, while the Colonel and Victoria were in Pittsburgh, she had another of her famous visions. She suddenly saw Demosthenes, always her favorite spirit, standing in front of her and ordering her to go to New York, to a house at 17 Jones Street. Victoria obeyed, and when she arrived she found the house exactly as Demosthenes had described it; in the library, waiting for her on a little table, was a copy of his *Orations*. It was all destiny, and the rest of the Claflins shortly recognized it for just that, and flocked to New York to join Victoria in her good fortune. And it was Buck Claflin, in his old riverman's way, who went to Commodore Vanderbilt and sold the old man on trying magnetic healing as a way of easing his various ailments. Tennessee took over, and even if Vanderbilt was not able to marry her she was able to persuade him to set herself and Victoria up in the brokerage business. It began on January 20, 1870, and Vanderbilt saw to it that representatives of every big financial house in New York came to the opening at 44 Broad Street. The sisters had cards engraved: "Woodhull, Claflin & Co." Soon they were so besieged that they became the "Bewitching Brokers" instead of just "She Brokers," and had to put a sign up in the vestibule: "All gentlemen will state their business and then retire at once." The Commodore's tips continued to increase their success, especially on Black Friday, in September 1870, when panic gripped Wall Street. With the whole Claflin brood in her increasing retinue of spiritualists followers, including Andrews now, Victoria took over as the mistress of a plush, gilt house at 15 East Thirty-Eighth Street, in the fashionable Murray Hill sector. There were about as many servants as there were dependents, but at least the servants kept order.

It was Victoria's bad luck that her family always embarrassed her at the most inopportune times. The weekly paper Vanderbilt had set up for Tennie and for her—Victoria soon took most of it over from her sister—was proving a perfect vehicle for the expression of her ideas and for those filtered through the minds of Andrews and Colonel Blood. *Woodhull and Claflin's Weekly* struck out against everything from bought love to bogus bonds and manipulations of the wealthy to defraud. It had begun to muckrack fearlessly, and almost all the rich men of the day were upbraided—except, of course, Commodore Vanderbilt. In certain respects, even he was not deferred to; the weekly published, for the first time in the United States, the English translation of the *Communist Manifesto* of Marx and Engels. Victoria and Tennie had become the two most spectacular members of Section 12 of the International Workingmen's Association, which Marx founded in 1864. As a center of American radicalism, the section was vocal and legitimate, though the more serious-minded immigrant Socialists from Europe did not especially approve of some of its profligate enthusiasms. Even so careful a man as Samuel Gompers had been impressed with Victoria Woodhull. Gompers, the first president of the American Federation of Labor, wrote that she was "dazzling New York by the brilliance of her oratory" and that her attractive personality and passionate advocacy of human freedom had made her a woman to be reckoned with as well as admired, despite her tendencies toward "irresponsible action." But, as Gompers also sadly noted, Mrs. Woodhull's repeated espousal of free love finally alienated her from the main body of the radical movement. She virtually made free love a part of her Presidential platform, urging that a woman fortunate enough to be caught up in "boundless love" should "consider superior offspring a necessity and . . . procreate only with superior men." It was shocking enough to read such things but Victoria, being Victoria, might have got away with it had there not occurred an especially distasteful airing of the Claflin ménage's dirty linen. It came only a few days after Mrs. Woodhull had taken another suffrage convention by storm, this one at Apollo Hall in New York, where she had cried out that if Congress did not grant women their rights, "We will overthrow this bogus Republic and plant a government of righteousness in its stead . . . We mean treason, we mean secession . . . We are plotting revolution." Even old Horace Greeley, who had never been much of a Woodhull fan, wrote a long editorial praising her for having the courage of her opinions, and recommending that others emulate her. Then Roxanna Claflin marched into Essex Police Court with all the vindictiveness of an angry mother-in-law, even though Victoria and Colonel Blood weren't legally married. One might properly compare her pique to that of Mrs. Morse against Theodore Tilton.

"I came here because I want to get my daughter out of this man's clutches," Roxanna shouted at the judge She added that Colonel Blood had threatened to kill her, that he spent money lavishly and that if it were not for him, Victoria and Tennessee, and obviously herself, "might be millionairesses." Roxanna thereupon leaned forward and fixed the judge balefully. "I say here and I call heaven to witness that there was the worst gang of free lovers in that house on Thirty-Eighth Street that ever lived. Stephen Pearl Andrews and Dr. Woodhull and lots more of such trash."

There was no shutting Roxanna up. Colonel Blood took the stand and denied that he had threatened his "mother-in-law" with more than a well-deserved spanking. But the Colonel was a little hazy about his and Victoria's liaison and about exactly who lived in the house on Thirty-Eighth Street, and under what circumstances.

Then Mrs. Woodhull came forward. She, too, denied that Colonel Blood had maltreated her mother; it was all the fault of another Claflin sister, Polly, and her husband, who were among the inmates of the house, and who sided with her mother in wanting to get Tennie Claflin and Victoria back on the road as an itinerant fortune-teller and spiritualist. Tennie was the next to testify, and she supported Victoria and Colonel Blood, who were her best friends, she said. "Since I was fourteen years old, I have kept thirty or thirty-five deadheads," she cried. "I have humbugged people, I know. But if I did it, it was to make money to keep these deadheads."

There was no decision in the case, possibly because there was nothing to decide, but the newspapers printed it all at length. Mrs. Woodhull was called everything from a "trance-physician" and "a brazen, snaky adventuress" to an "unsexed woman." It may have been the last that hurt most. Although her Presidential candidacy was not torpedoed, her formal alliance with the suffragists was critically shaken. As the two wings of the suffrage movement met together to censure those women who had endorsed Mrs. Woodhull, and at least by inference her free-love doctrine, Elizabeth Cady Stanton did her best to stem the opprobrium by blaming men for everything. "When the men who make the laws for us in Washington can stand forth and declare themselves pure and unspotted from all the sins mentioned in the Decalogue," said spunky Mrs. Stanton, "then we will demand that every woman who makes a consti-tutional argument on our platform shall be as chaste as Diana." Mrs. Woodhull's "face, manner and conversation all indicate the triumph of the moral, intellectual and spiritual," she went on. "We have had enough women sacrificed to this sentimental, hypocritical prating about purity. This is one of man's most effective engines for our division and subjugation . . . Let us henceforth stand by womanhood. If Victoria Woodhull must be crucified, let men drive the spikes and plait the crown of thorns."

It was a brave enough defense, but Victoria had made her own decision by now anyway. What counted with her was the main battle—against moral sham. She decided she would rather be right than President. And she sat down and wrote her letter to the *World* and summoned Theodore Tilton to her office.

There was a quality of destiny in their being brought together. If their meeting was prompted by his deep adversity, and her momentary one, it fittingly joined the injured boy romantic to the boldest woman in America, who was in a position to utilize his hurt to her advantage and to what she thought, or at least professed to think, was his. It would be Mrs. Woodhull who would have the courage of Tilton's romanticism; and even if things were not to turn out quite as he wanted, she would manage to do what he was aiming to do all along, despite his disclaimers—strike Beecher "to the heart," as he ultimately admitted, for the wrong the pastor had done him.

CHAPTER IX

Where Victoria Woodhull's belief in Progress, with a capital P, drove her reluctantly ahead, letting the devil take the hindmost, the devil to Theodore Tilton, tormented and guilt-ridden as he was about some of his un-Godly opinions, remained a ghost always loitering in the background. In many ways, because he regarded himself as a faster talker than the devil and could more readily rationalize himself out of predicaments, and even out of sin, Henry Ward Beecher was closer to Victoria than Tilton was.

No man, after he had listened to her recitation of the scandal in his home, became a more effective engine of elevation for Mrs. Woodhull, however, than Tilton. The first thing he did was rush to tell his friend Frank Moulton what had happened. The next day, May 23, he and Moulton returned to have a talk with Mrs. Woodhull. They discussed the scandal allegations briefly, but Mrs. Woodhull mostly gave the two gentlemen "an extravagant account of her views on spiritualism," Tilton later said. "She stood in the middle of the floor and built a kind of ladder with her hands between the earth and the heavens, on which she said the angels ascended and descended, that there was communication between the two worlds." Moulton tried to point out to her that the "cruel story" she had alluded to might hurt decent persons, such as

Mrs. Tilton, and "The Woodhull" was thereupon invited both to the Tilton home and the Moulton home, over the protests of the respective wives, to see for herself what fine, moral women they were. Elizabeth Tilton hated everything Mrs. Woodhull stood for, but she tried hard to be nice to Victoria and even gave her a book of poems.

Tilton and Moulton quickly went to see Beecher, too. The preacher, according to what both men said later, agreed that Mrs. Woodhull must be mollified, and that Tilton should be the chief mollifier. "Mr. Beecher said he would very cheerfully co-operate in that plan," Tilton said, indicating the agreement among the three of them "to treat her with kindness . . . as a gentleman should treat a lady." The preacher, in his subsequent testimony, denied he had become part of a conspiracy to silence Mrs. Woodhull, but he was caught in a web of his usual inconsistencies. At one point he declared: "She never in any way whatever, by my counsel, was brought into this matter, nor did I propose any counsel, method, mode, machinery or anything else for the use of her . . . Mr. Moulton and Mr. Tilton told me that they regarded her as one of the most extraordinary women they had ever met, and that, surrounded as she was by bad influences, she acted from the lower plane of her nature, that if she could be put into communication with the upper influences of life, and her noble nature appealed to, they thought she would lead a revolution in the times in which she lived, and their eulogies were simply extravagant of her. I never counseled her association with Elizabeth Tilton nor with Emma Moulton—a world too good. I never thought of her coming to my house." But when he was asked if he had not approved of Tilton establishing "pleasant relations" with Mrs. Woodhull so that a further blow of publicity from her might be averted, Beecher replied: "I thought . . . it was not an improper thing to do." And the pastor admitted he might have thanked Tilton for the "interference."

Tilton took to his job of pacifying Victoria Woodhull with his customary ardor and zeal. As usual, he overdid it. In an early issue of the *Golden Age* he wrote: "If the woman's movement has a Joan of Arc, it is this gentle but fiery genius . . . Her bold social theories have startled many good souls, but anybody who on this account imagines her to stand below the whitest and purest of her sex will misplace a woman who in moral integrity rises to the full height of the highest." In a creative frenzy, he recast her suffrage memorial to Congress for popular distribution and then wrote her biography from a series of disconnected notes handed him by Colonel Blood. When he gave her the first draft, Mrs. Woodhull was disappointed. "You have left out the most important parts," she told Tilton, indicating some of her proudest accomplishments, including her claim that she had brought her idiot son back to life after he seemed to be dead for two hours. "To write my life and leave out that incident would be to play *Hamlet* with the part of Hamlet omitted," she cried. So Tilton worked through another long night, putting in that and other details of her apostolic powers to heal the sick and her spiritual liaison with Demosthenes. When he showed her the revised version, Victoria was pleased, and the biography was published as a special *Golden Age Tract*.

Tilton began seeing a great deal of Mrs. Woodhull. They went rowing and to Coney Island together, and he passed a lot of time at her house on Thirty-Eighth Street. There was no doubt that his admiration for her began to overleap his ulterior motives. Where he took credit for holding her back, she later insisted that "months of friendly intercourse" made him "magnanimous and grand" and she saw him "playing a great role in the social revolution," though "I never could induce him to stand wholly and unreservedly, and on principle, upon the free love platform, and I always, therefore, feared that he might for a time vacillate or go backward." The degree of intimacy between them was to become a much debated point, and Mrs. Woodhull herself seemed to enjoy adding to the confusion. She once told a reporter from a Chicago paper that "I ought to know Mr. Tilton, for he was my devoted lover for more than half a year."

"Do I understand, dear madam, that the fascination was mutual and irresistible?" the scribe asked.

Mrs. Woodhull replied that "so enamored and infatuated were we with each other that for three months we were hardly out of each other's sights, and he slept every night in my arms." But when she reached New York, she told another inquiring journalist: "Why, I am not a fool. A woman who is before the world as I am would not make such a flagrant statement, even if it were true." Confusing or not, it was all quite titillating.

Mrs. Woodhull's influence over Beecher was somewhat less successful, though their relations remain hazy in detail. Phrenologically speaking, in the mystic language of Stephen Pearl Andrews, she credited the pastor with "Amativeness 8," on a scale of one, which simply meant that she thought he had a lot of sex appeal. Beecher insisted he saw Mrs. Woodhull only a few times, at a yacht race, accidentally once at the Tiltons', and at a dinner following a reception. There was another meeting the preacher admitted to, but his description of it varied considerably from hers. After what she termed many friendly discussions and a correspondence "that was not one of mere platonic affection," she wrote him a letter on November 19, 1871, asking him to introduce her the following evening at Steinway Hall, in Brooklyn, where she was making a major speech. It was more than a favor she was asking: it was a warning, and it pointed up the fact that, ultimately, the failure of the campaign to silence Mrs. Woodhull was chiefly Beecher's fault.

Typically, there was irony involved. Beecher's family, his brothers, sisters, and half-sisters, had always differed violently and publicly over most urgent questions of the day. Where Beecher and Isabella Beecher Hooker, still an admirer of Mrs. Woodhull's, were usually abreast of social change, Harriet Beecher Stowe and the indomitable Catherine Beecher were more wary. Of all his sisters, the pastor felt himself closest to Mrs. Stowe. Both to her and to Catherine Beecher, Victoria Woodhull was the personification of a "She Devil." Catherine had already made her feelings about "The Woodhull" clear, but Mrs. Stowe was now also joining the fray. In Beecher's religious weekly, the *Christian Union*, a series of critical attacks against Victoria Woodhull ran under her name, and then came a serialized novel containing a satiric portrait of a woman who could not possibly be meant to be anyone but Mrs. Woodhull.

Tilton tried his best to hold back Mrs. Woodhull's anger. "Now, if you wish to answer Mrs. Stowe's attack," he said, "do it in a way of superior gracefulness, gentleness and charity." These were three qualities Victoria scarcely had, but she managed to lean over backward and make a kindly reference to Beecher in *Woodhull and Claflin's Weekly.* Her momentary temperance waned. She saw her Steinway Hall speech as a proper challenge to throw at the pastor, and she wrote him:

> DEAR SIR: For reasons in which *you* are deeply interested, as well as myself and the cause of truth, I desire to have an interview with you, without fail, at some hour tomorrow. Two of your sisters have gone out of their way to assail my character and purposes, both by the means of the public press, and by numerous private letters written to various persons with whom they seek to injure me, and thus to defeat the political ends at which I aim.
>
> You doubtless know that it is within my power to strike back, and in ways more disastrous than anything that can come to me; but *I* do not desire to do this. I simply desire justice from those from whom I have a right to expect it. I speak guardedly, but I think you will understand me. I repeat that I must have an interview tomorrow, since I am to speak tomorrow evening at Steinway Hall; and what I say or shall not say will depend largely upon the result of the interview.
>
> Yours very truly,
>
> VICTORIA C. WOODHULL

P. S.—Please return answer by bearer.

It was Frank Moulton, logically enough, who arranged an interview between Mrs. Woodhull and Beecher the following day. Both Moulton and Tilton urged Beecher to preside at the meeting, for obvious reasons, but Beecher was adamant. He told Mrs. Woodhull that he sympathized with her views on woman suffrage, but could not introduce her because of the other opinions she held. As he later put it, "As I understood she was about to avow doctrines which I abhor, I would not be induced to give her public countenance."

Mrs. Woodhull's version was far more graphic. Beecher, she said, admitted he was "a moral coward on the subject" of free love, even though "he agreed with nearly all my views on the question." She insisted he told her that "marriage was 'the grave of love' and that he never married a couple that he did not 'feel condemned,'" but that, even if he was twenty years ahead of his church on the subject, he could not preach what he felt because, "'if I were to do so, I should preach to empty seats and it would be the ruin of my church.'" Beecher, Mrs. Woodhull said, "got up on the sofa on his knees beside me, and taking my face between his hands, while the tears streamed down his cheeks, he begged me to let him off." Whether she was right or wrong, it was a fact that the pastor was forever having to deny such postures.

Theodore Tilton, in his quaint, heroic, romantic way, filled the breach. The night of November 20 was stormy, but a large crowd turned out at Steinway Hall. The subject of Mrs. Woodhull's speech was "The Principles of Social Freedom, Involving the Question of Free Love, Marriage, Divorce, and Prostitution." It was all "for the express purpose," Victoria made clear, "of silencing the voices and stopping the pens of those who, either ignorantly or willfully, persistently misrepresent, slander, abuse and vilify [me] on account of [my] outspoken advocacy of, and supreme faith in, God's first and best law. . ." Nobody, it seemed, was going to perform the rites of introduction. Tilton later swore that he and Moulton "had no intention of going" to the hall, but that they went at the last moment. He said he found Mrs. Woodhull "weeping" in an anteroom because "she said she did not believe there was a courageous man on the face of the earth." For Tilton this served as a challenge, and he dashed out onto the platform and, declaring that he had happened "to have an unoccupied night . . . five minutes ago I did not expect to be here," he introduced Mrs. Woodhull in his best lecture-platform manner. "It may be that she is a fanatic," he said, "it may be that I am a fool. But, before high heaven, I would rather be both fanatic and fool in one than to be such a coward as would deny a woman the right of free speech."

Victoria Woodhull was in rare form. "All compelling laws of marriage are despotic," she cried, "remnants of the barbaric age in which they were originated . . . All that is good and commendable would continue to exist if all marriage laws were repealed tomorrow. . ." There was a demonstration of mixed applause and hissing when one of Victoria's sisters, Utica Hooker, arose in a stage box and sweetly asked: "How would you like to come into this world without knowing who your father or your mother were?" When someone shouted: "Are you a free lover?" Victoria became a ball of flashing fire. "Yes! I am a free lover," she cried back. "I have an inalienable, con- stitutional, and natural right to love whom I may, to love as long or as short a period as I can, to change that love every day if I please . . . I have a further right to demand a free unrestricted exercise of that right, and it is your duty not only to accord it, but as a community to see that I am protected in it. I trust that I am fully understood, for I mean just that and nothing else . . . Promiscuity in sexuality is simply the anar- chical stage of development wherein the passions rule supreme. When spirituality comes in and rescues the real man or woman from the domain of the purely material, promiscuity is simply impossible."

The speech was a great success in fanning controversy. As Theodore Tilton sat on the platform listening to it, it was a success for another reason. By his gracious act of introduction, he had at least postponed disaster, for Mrs. Woodhull had left out her prime example of what she regarded as the hypocritical practice of free love—the adultery of Henry Ward Beecher and Mrs. Tilton and the foolish attempt to deny it. It would be almost a year before Mrs. Woodhull would finally break the story. In the meantime, Beecher and the Tiltons went through

"GET THEE BEHIND ME (MRS.) SATAN"

*Thomas Nast's famous cartoon depicting the wickedness of
Victoria Woodhull.*

more soul-torture, enough to make all of them, but especially Beecher, wish that it were all over, to hope, in fact, for death.

Tilton's mother-in-law, Mrs. Morse, who had done so much to start the scandal ball rolling, was as meddlesome as ever. She had just written another of her mad letters to the preacher. It was in this one that she addressed him as "My Dear Son," and asked for money to help pay the bills for herself and for Elizabeth Tilton. "Do come and see me," she begged. "I will promise that the secret of her life, as she [Mrs. Tilton] calls it, shall not be mentioned. I know it is hard to bring it up, as you must have suffered intensely as we all will, I fear, 'till released by death. Do you pray for me? If not, please do. I never felt more rebellious than now, more in need of God's and human help. Do you know I think it strange that you should ask me to call you son? I felt . . . you would be to me all this endearing name. Am I mistaken?" She signed herself "Mother." Beecher did not reply. He gave the letter to Frank Moulton to keep, along with all the rest.

If Tilton's act of heroism in introducing Mrs. Woodhull at Steinway Hall in the face of Beecher's cowardice had staved off the worst, it sorely hurt his reputation as a lecturer. His continuing association with "The Woodhull" and his non-attendance at Plymouth Church also combined to raise a ruckus among some members of the church. Beecher, with his usual prescience, tried to get Tilton quietly to resign, so his name could be removed from the rolls. The pastor sent Moulton a letter on the subject. "We do not want to run the risk of complications which, in such a body, no man can foresee, and no one control," he wrote. "Once free from a sense of responsibility for *him* . . . there would be a strong tendency for a kindly feeling to set in. . ." Tilton would have none of it. He refused to request a dismissal.

Beecher had not seen much of Elizabeth Tilton in recent months, but now he managed a few short, secret walks with her, and he wrote her a prayer in which he said: "This world ceases to hold me as it did. I live in the thought and the hope of the coming immortality, and seem to myself most of the time to be standing on the edge of the other life, wondering whether I may not at any time hear the call to 'Come up hither.'" He added: "I shall be in New Haven next week to begin my course of lectures to the theological class on preaching. My wife takes the boat for Havana and Florida on Thursday. I called on Wednesday, but you were out. . ." When he was later asked: "What made you think she would be interested to know you were going to New Haven?" he replied: "Well, I flattered myself it would be interesting to almost anybody to know I was going to deliver a course of lectures at Yale." As for the Havana information, he said: "Well, just at that time it was the most interesting fact, almost, that I had, and I naturally would impart it to a friend." But he was admittedly afraid to see Mrs. Tilton alone any more, indoors anyway. "I never allowed myself to talk with her on anything but religious topics," he was to explain.

The preacher's fits of melancholy took expression in constant unburdenings to Moulton. One long epistle in particular, which became known as "The Ragged Edge Letter," grew to be famous. He wrote it early in 1872:

> MY DEAR FRIEND: To *say* that I have a church on my hands is simple enough—but to have the hundreds and thousands of men pressing me, each one with his keen suspicion, or anxiety, or zeal; to see tendencies which, if not stopped, would break out into a ruinous defense of me; to stop them without seeming to do it; to prevent anyone questioning me; to meet and allay prejudices against T. which had their beginning years before this; to keep serene as if I were not alarmed or disturbed; to be cheerful at home and among friends when I was suffering the torments of the damned; to pass sleepless nights often, and yet to come up fresh and full for Sunday—all this may be talked about, but the real thing cannot be understood from the outside, nor its wearing and grinding on the nervous system . . . If my destruction would place him [Tilton] all right, that

shall not stand in the way. I am willing to step down and out. No one can offer more than that. That I do offer. Sacrifice me without hesitation, if you can clearly see your way to his safety and happiness thereby. I do not think that anything would be gained by it. I should be destroyed, but he would not be saved. E. and the children would have their future clouded. In one point of view I could desire the sacrifice on my part. Nothing could possibly be so bad as the horror of the great darkness in which I spend much of my time. I look upon death as sweeter-faced than any friend I have in the world. Life would be pleasant if I could see that re-built which is shattered. But to live on the sharp and ragged edge of anxiety, remorse, fear, despair, and yet to put on all the appearance of serenity and happiness, cannot be endured much longer . . .

This was only the first of several declarations of Beecher's willingness to resign, a seemingly harsh sacrifice for a man of

THE SKELETON IN THE PLYMOUTH CLOSET

his national prestige if he was guilty only of having incited an undue affection in one of his parishioners. Both Tilton and Moulton from time to time picked him up on the suggestion, but whenever they suggested it Beecher demurred. The year 1872 marked the twenty-fifth anniversary of Beecher's establishment in the pulpit of Plymouth Church, and since the pastor was still writing the life of Christ, in several volumes, Tilton pointed out that he might logically take an extended trip to the Holy Land. "You will never have such an opportunity to resign amid the world's good opinion as now," Tilton said. "It can be known to all the world that you have gone to see with your own eyes the footprints of the Master whose life you are now writing." It was a persuasive argument and Beecher said he would think it over; but he never mentioned it again. One thing had become apparent, however: each man wanted the other out of the church and out of the way. All the protestations made by both, the mouthings of renewed friendship, had become sham.

Victoria Woodhull, after her Steinway Hall speech, continued to widen her horizons. She repeated the same address in staid Boston, where the catcalls and the applause were also evenly mixed, and her notoriety was increased. At the new convention of the National Suffrage Association she once again appeared on the stage with Mrs. Stanton, Mrs. Hooker, and Miss Anthony, but Miss Anthony made it clear that they would follow Mrs. Woodhull only on suffrage matters, not on free love, spiritualism or some other things she was espousing, such as Communism and the causes of the International Workingmen's Association. A lecture Mrs. Woodhull gave on "The Impending Revolution," in which she attacked Commodore Vanderbilt as well as other wealthy men who allegedly persecuted and robbed the poor, helped widen the breach between herself and the women who had lent her their support.

The break came in May, and it was Susan Anthony who provoked it. As she put it, "Mrs. Woodhull has the advantage of us because she has the newspaper, and she persistently means to run our craft into her port and none other. If she were influenced by women spirits I might consent to be a mere sail-hoister for her, but as it is she is wholly owned and dominated by men spirits, and I spurn the control of the whole lot of them." When Mrs. Woodhull, in behalf of "The People's Party," tried to invade and take over an anniversary meeting of the suffrage association at Steinway Hall, Miss Anthony ordered the gas turned off. So "The People's Party" rented the Apollo Theater, and on May 10, 1872, summoned "all male and female beings of America" to come together.

An assorted group of communists, spiritualists, free lovers, and some suffragists, numbering five hundred in all, gathered and nominated Victoria Woodhull for President under the formal banner of "The Equal Rights Party." Frederick Douglass, the Negro reform leader, was chosen to be her running-mate. Mrs. Woodhull made a glorious, impassioned keynote speech. "Who will dare to attempt to unlock the luminous portals of the future with the rusty key of the past?" she cried. The applause was deafening. There was a ratification meeting the next month at Cooper Union, and to the tune of "Comin' Thro' the Rye" a rousing campaign song was sung:

> *Yes! Victoria we've selected*
> *For our chosen head:*
> *With Fred Douglass on the ticket*
> *We will raise the dead.*
> *Then around them let us rally*
> *Without fear or dread,*
> *And next March we'll put the Grundys*
> *In their little bed.*

Now the real persecution of Victoria Woodhull began. Because of the views they held, the Claflin brood was forced to leave the new house they had moved to on Twenty-Third Street. Commodore Vanderbilt, his hand severely bitten by those whom he had fed, withdrew his support from *Woodhull and Claflin's Weekly*, and Mrs. Woodhull and her sister were forced out of their business office when the rent was raised. Victoria asked Beecher to help her find a place to live—even the hotels refused to accept her—but Beecher politely said he could do nothing. Faced with financial ruin, the sisters resorted to an old device, a popular practice of the day—blackmail. They threatened to expose certain secrets in the lives of prominent persons. No figures were immediately mentioned, but the implication was obvious. Among the publications Mrs. Woodhull talked about was a scandalous little brochure she got up called *Tit for Tat*, which promised her a way of revenge against the leaders of the suffrage movement who had abandoned her. There was not very much to be said derogatorily about Miss Anthony, but some of the other ladies were more vulnerable. Nothing actually was ever published, but some proof-sheets were strategically distributed, and a few hints dropped.

When Theodore Tilton heard about it, he was enraged at this smearing of old friends, and he bluntly told Mrs. Woodhull how he felt. They had a violent quarrel. She later insisted the real cause of their break was Tilton's support of Horace Greeley for the Presidency instead of her. Probably both explanations were correct. In any event, their friendship was over. Tilton's backing of Greeley simply hurt the great editor, lending his candidacy a tinge of "free love-ism," something he had always violently fought in his newspaper. Clairvoyantly, Mrs. Woodhull told Tilton that "I see a coffin following you out to Cincinnati," where the Republican convention was held, and she predicted Tilton's responsibility for Greeley's death. It may not have been as close as that, but at the end of November, a tragic, broken, and demented figure, Horace Greeley died.

A month earlier, tired, worn, and discouraged herself, and many thought also mad, Victoria Woodhull began her final revenge against her detractors and against those, such as Tilton, who had forsaken her. She broke the Beecher-Tilton scandal wide open.

At a spiritualist convention in Boston, representing herself as "mere nuncio to the world of the facts that have happened," she related in "a rhapsody of indignant eloquence" the details of the case and prophesied "the bearing of those events upon the future of spiritualism." She spoke, as usual, "in a trance," and later said: "They tell me that I used some naughty words upon that occasion, but all I know is that if I swore *I did not swear profanely*, and some said, with tears streaming from their eyes, that *I swore divinely*." Whichever way she swore, Boston was typically shocked into suppressing the story. Mrs. Woodhull thereupon repeated it to certain reporters from New York, whose editors also held it back, prompting her to sneer that "an impecunious reporter can be bought off with a few hundred dollars." Finally, in the issue of her own *Weekly* of November 2, 1872, she printed what she said was a verbatim report of one of the quashed interviews.

After embellishing the facts of the scandal with her own fancy, Mrs. Woodhull declared:

> I am impelled by no hostility whatever to Mr. Beecher, nor by any personal pique toward him or any other person . . . The immense physical potency of Mr. Beecher and the indomitable urgency of his great nature for the intimacy and embraces of the noble and cultured women about him, instead of being a bad thing as the world thinks, or thinks it thinks, or professes to think that it thinks, is one of the grandest and noblest of the endowments of this truly great and representative man . . . Every great man of Mr. Beecher's type has in the past, and will ever have the need for, and the right to, the loving manifestations of many women . . . It is the paradox of my position that, believing in the right of privacy and in the perfect right of Mr. Beecher, socially, morally and divinely, to have sought the embraces of Mrs. Tilton . . . I still invade the most secret and sacred affairs of his life and expose them . . . But the case is exceptional, and what I do I do for a great purpose. The social world is in the very agony of its new birth . . . the leaders of progress are in the very act of storming the last fortress of bigotry and error. Somebody must be hurled into the gap, and I have the power to think and compel Mr. Beecher to go forward and to do the duty for

humanity from which he shrinks . . . Whether he sinks or swims in the fiery trial, the agitation by which truth is evolved will have been promoted.

The only evil, Mrs. Woodhull thundered, lay in the "false and artificial belief" that "lovers own their lovers, husbands their wives, and that they have the right to spy over and to interfere" with each other. "I conceive that Mrs. Tilton's love for Mr. Beecher was her true marriage . . . and that her marriage to Mr. Tilton is prostitution," and neither Tilton nor Mrs. Beecher, she added, had any more right to criticize their respective mates' carnal activity "than they have a right to know what I ate for breakfast." Beecher's "amative nature is good," she said, and while the "sheer impertinence" of morality had made him "a poltroon, a coward and a sneak for failing to stand shoulder to shoulder with me," he "is in heart, in conviction and in life an ultra-socialist reformer" and "the fault with which I charge him is not infidelity to the old ideas, but unfaithfulness to the new. . ."

When the reporter in the account of the interview asked: "Do you mean to say that Mr. Beecher disapproves of the present marriage system?" Mrs. Woodhull quoted the preacher on what she claimed he had told her at the time of his refusal to sponsor her at Steinway Hall, that he shuddered at the marriage ceremony but could not speak his mind because "it would be the ruin of my church." She also said that Beecher told her: "We shall never have a better state until children are begotten and bred on the scientific plan." Mrs. Woodhull said she had expressed her contempt for the preacher's cowardice by telling him: "Then you are as big a fraud as any time-serving preacher. A sorry pass this Christian country has come to, paying forty thousand preachers to lie to it from Sunday to Sunday." The reporter Mrs. Woodhull quoted thereupon observed: "It seems you took a good deal of pains to draw Mr. Beecher out. . ."

By not hugging the Tiltons quite so closely to her bosom, Mrs. Woodhull dealt more lightly with them, but her contempt was still apparent. She simply accused Mrs. Tilton of having "the sentiment of the real slaveholder" because she had been upset that her "reverend paramour" had been unfaithful to her by having other mistresses too. Tilton was dismissed like a child for having exhibited "maudlin sentiment and mock heroics and 'dreadful suzz.'" Mrs. Woodhull said she had pointed out to him that "he was not exactly a vestal virgin himself" and told him that he had been "humbugged all his life" by "Sunday school morality and pulpit pharaiseeism." The reporter commented: "You speak like some weird prophetess, madam." Mrs. Woodhull replied: "I am a prophetess, I am an evangel—I am a Saviour, if you would but see it, but I too come not to bring peace but a sword."

It was her intention, Mrs. Woodhull said, that "this article shall burst like a bombshell into the ranks of the moralistic social camp." It did, though not exactly as she had expected. More than a hundred thousand copies of the *Weekly* sold out, and the demand so far exceeded the supply that secondhand copies eventually went for ten dollars and one man admitted he had paid forty dollars. Overnight, the scandal became the talk of the town, and then of the country.

Despite the date of issue, the *Weekly*'s story appeared on the streets five days earlier, on October 28. At one o'clock in the morning, the leading suppressor of vice in New York, a young dry-goods salesman named Anthony Comstock, who was chief vice-warden for the Young Men's Christian Association, saw it. Ten hours later, armed with a wealth of evidence against Mrs. Woodhull and Tennie Claflin, he went to the office of the District Attorney of New York County, who promised that a warrant for the arrest of the sisters would be issued. Comstock didn't wait. He suddenly remembered that Congress had just passed a statute making the sending of obscene material through the mails a misdemeanor, and he went to see the Federal authorities. Within an hour two United States marshals intercepted Mrs. Woodhull and Miss Claflin as they were riding down Broad Street in a carriage with five hundred copies of the *Weekly* on the carriage floor.

Mrs. Woodhull later said that "the U.S. government treated Woodhull and Claflin with endearing familiarity. It sat on their laps on the way to court."

The sisters were taken to United States Circuit Court. Both of them were sedately dressed in black, and they sat in the center of the courtroom as the United States Attorney asked they be held in $10,000 bail each because they had not only violated the mail laws but "have been guilty of a most abominable and unjust charge against one of the purest and best citizens of . . . the United States . . . whose character is well worth-while the Government of the United States to vindicate." The court said $8,000 would be sufficient. The town's best-known eccentric, a man named George Francis Train, who had opposed the sisters before, now rushed to their rescue. He offered to pay the $16,000, but Mrs. Woodhull's counsel advised that she and Tennessee might as well go to the relatively comfortable Ludlow Street jail and wait until events took their course, by which he meant other suits might be filed and martyrdom more fully established. Mrs. Woodhull agreed. She and Tennie marched off to jail crying that their arrest was "a bastard New York monstrosity begotten of lust, fear and guilt." It set the tone for what followed.

The following day, after Grand Jury indictments against the sisters had been handed up, they again appeared in court, this time with the eminent and colorful attorney, William F. Howe, of Howe & Hummel, representing them, in a purple vest and plaid pantaloons. Howe pointed out, before the sisters were arrested on the new bench warrants and returned to Ludlow Street jail, that what they had printed in the *Weekly* was no more obscene than some things that were said in the Bible. This may have given George Francis Train his cue, for Train thereupon published a little paper of his own, called *Train Ligue*, through which he scattered quotations from the Old Testament under scandalous headlines. He finally had his minor martyrdom when he, too, was arrested and thrown into the far more uncomfortable Tombs, where he remained for a time on principle, refusing bail.

On the morning of November 5, which was election day, with Victoria Woodhull, the nominee of the Equal Rights Party, languishing behind bars, Theodore Tilton returned to Brooklyn from a campaign tour in behalf of Horace Greeley in New England. "As soon as I entered the house," he later said, "Mrs. Tilton, with great distress, put into my hands a copy of *Woodhull and Claflin's Weekly*, which was the first knowledge I had of the publication of the story." Having hastily read it, Tilton rushed over to see Frank Moulton, and then they both met with Henry Ward Beecher, who subsequently insisted he had not read the scandal story, not even when he was fore-warned of it by "a tall, thin, lank old gentleman of about sixty years of age, who came to tell me that there was an awful thing a-going to be published." As the three men discussed what should now be done, they agreed that the best course was to continue, insofar as they could, "the policy of silence." Under the circumstances, it was about as visionary a course as some of Victoria Woodhull's spirit-sallies.

CHAPTER X

The crowds at Plymouth Church were just as great, if anything greater, now that the famous pastor's eloquent Gospel of Love was spiced by the piquant sauce of scandal. Outwardly, Beecher remained the benevolent, white-maned incarnation of righteousness. When a friend stopped him on the street to inquire about the "outrage" Victoria Woodhull had perpetrated, and stated, rather than asked: "Of course, Mr. Beecher, the whole thing is a fraud from beginning to end," Beecher looked his idolator in the eye and replied firmly: "Entirely!" To Elizabeth Tilton, worried sick about the scandal, the preacher wrote consolingly: "Every pure woman on earth will feel that this wanton and unprovoked assault is aimed at you, but reaches to universal womanhood," and he told her that God would protect her, that "the rain that beats down the flower to the earth will pass at length, and the stem, bent but not broken, will rise again and blossom as before." But he took no action against Victoria Woodhull, who had dared him to sue her for libel.

After remaining in jail for a month, Mrs. Woodhull and her sister were freed on bail supplied by two of her admirers. By now, the newspapers of the country had, in their steady stream of editorials on the scandal, begun to fall into two fairly distinct camps. There were those that believed nothing—hell, damnation or the Tombs—would be too bad for "The Woodhull." But some of the most influential papers in the land came to her aid and support, not because they approved of her views but because they maintained that the persecution to which she was being subjected was a firm violation of the freedom of the press.

The case was complicated by another libel action brought concurrently against Mrs. Woodhull and her *Weekly*. Over the next several months, she and Tennie Claflin were in and out of jail so often on both cases that practically everyone lost count. Constant hearings in various courts were held, all of them attended by curious crowds. An eminent battery of attorneys, led by Howe & Hummel—no one could tell who was paying for them, unless it was the eccentric and wealthy George Francis Train—defended the two women. Howe quoted volubly from the Bible to prove that the obscenity charge on which the case had been based had a holy writ to sustain its proper application. Hummel cited Smollett, and others dipped into Shakespeare. Between arrests, Mrs. Woodhull continued to attack Beecher and Tilton in *Woodhull and Claflin's Weekly*, which came out irregularly, its issuance depending chiefly on the physical whereabouts of its editors. When she was periodically at liberty Victoria traveled around the country lecturing on "The Naked Truth." At one point she suffered what appeared to be a heart attack, but it turned out to be only a ruptured blood vessel, and she was up and about in a few days, after numerous obituary editorials about "the wicked Woodhull" had already been published.

Spiritualists everywhere hailed her as a martyr, but the suffragists were not so unanimous. Nevertheless, they accepted her limited martyrdom on matters of female emancipation; the "Woodhull Memorial" the canny lawyer Benjamin Butler had written for Victoria to deliver in Congress was still recognized at conventions, even if Victoria Woodhull was no longer invited. Susan Anthony insisted on her right to vote under the memorial and the Fourteenth Amendment; indicted, tried, and found guilty of fraud, she refused to pay the hundred-dollar fine levied against her, insisting proudly that "resistance to tyranny is obedience to God," and was finally set free, victorious.

It was Benjamin Butler who at length paved the way for Mrs. Woodhull's clearance, six months after she had been taken into custody on the Beecher-Tilton case. Butler wrote an open letter in which he pointed out, as a member of the Congressional committee that had drawn up the obscenity statute, that it did not cover what Mrs. Woodhull had allegedly done. "The statute was meant to cover . . . the sending that class of lithographs, prints, engravings, licentious books and other matters which are published by bad men for the purpose of the corruption of youth, through the United States mail. . ." When the case was finally tried, the court, agreed with Butler that the "other matters" in the law did not cover weekly newspapers, and the jury acquitted Victoria Woodhull and Tennessee Claflin.

As far as Beecher and the Tiltons were concerned, however, the damage had been done. The preacher's outward poise, in particular, no longer hid his inner turmoil. In spite of the determination to meet Mrs. Woodhull's threat with silence, it was not long before Beecher suggested, at one of the meetings he and Tilton held with Moulton, that Tilton write a "card" to the newspapers, repenting his earlier association with "The Woodhull." Beecher even drafted such a letter for Tilton. "In an unguarded enthusiasm, I hoped well and much of one who has proved utterly unprincipled," it said. "I shall never again notice her stories, and now utterly repudiate her statements made concerning me and mine." The suggestion made Tilton "very angry," and he curtly reminded Beecher that the pastor "knew very well that my relations with Mrs. Woodhull had not been prompted by an unguarded enthusiasm; that I had gone to Mrs. Woodhull deliberately, and by design," and that Beecher had been "a partner in that design."

Beecher's family remained a problem. His obstreperous half-sister Isabella Beecher Hooker wrote to him from Hartford, urging him to tell the truth and come out wholeheartedly for "free love," as Victoria Woodhull had suggested.

When Mrs. Hooker offered to come down to Brooklyn and take charge of one of his services because "it seems to me God has been preparing me for this work, and you also, for years and years," Beecher was almost beside himself. He summoned Harriet Beecher Stowe and stationed her in a front pew at Plymouth Church every Sunday to make sure her "mad" half-sister would not suddenly appear. And, of all people, he sent Theodore Tilton up to Hartford to see Mrs. Hooker personally, because Tilton knew something about a past adultery in Mrs. Hooker's life which might help win her silence. The preacher himself wrote Mrs. Hooker, of the Woodhull tales: "I tread the falsehoods into the dirt from which they spring and go on my way rejoicing." He added that "the Lord has a pavilion in which he hides me until the storm is overpast" and spoke of "the barbarity of dragging a poor dear child of a woman [Mrs. Tilton] into this slough." Mrs. Hooker wrote her brother Thomas, a pastor in the West: "Now, Tom, so far as I can see, it is he who has dragged the dear child into the slough, and left her there." Thomas Beecher replied with alacrity. Mrs. Woodhull, he said, "only carries out Henry's philosophy, against which I recorded my philosophy twenty years ago . . . I cannot help him except by prayer . . . In my judgment, Henry is following the slippery doctrines of expediency . . . Of the two, Woodhull is my hero and Henry my coward, *as at present advised.* But I protest against the whole batch and all its belongings."

Tilton, like Beecher, was rapidly reaching the end of his rope. He wanted to shield his own family and avoid labeling himself publicly a cuckold, and he was still willing to shield Beecher for those reasons; but he also wanted the record set straight—to the extent at least that Beecher had done him a great injury. Both men, in tentative alliance one day, then out to save their own skins the next, became as skittish for the man in the middle, Moulton, to handle as marionettes on crossed strings. Endless conferences were held at which Moulton vainly offered pacifying prescriptions, and at which Elizabeth Tilton, looking more frail and birdlike than ever, sometimes sat in as a sort of half-forgotten tragic muse. The English language was tortuously twisted in the effort to make sexual intercourse out to be only "unhandsome advances" or something else that hung in tenuous verbalism between platonic yearning and the anxious bed. Tilton, after Mrs. Woodhull's story appeared, wrote for his own use several versions of what came to be called "The True Story" of the whole affair. He bound one treatment in a leather volume and showed it to friends.

For further "advice" he finally went to the Reverend Richard Storrs, next to Beecher the most prominent pastor in Brooklyn, and carried with him a statement from Mrs. Tilton which they had painfully worked out together. It quaintly set forth that "in July, 1870, prompted by my duty, I informed my husband that H. W. Beecher, my friend and pastor, had solicited me to be a wife to him, together with all that this implied." Dr. Storrs, who had been a close friend of Beecher's for many years, was shocked at the news Tilton brought him, and for the first time an outside preacher began to have real suspicions about the Plymouth Church pastor. When Tilton told Beecher what he had done, Beecher moaned: "Oh, Theodore, of all the men in the world, I wish you had kept clear of Dr. Storrs!" Tilton wanted to embody his wife's newest description of her intimacy with her pastor in a statement, and he told Beecher: "If you can stand that, you can stand the rest." Beecher, according to Tilton, replied, "You might as well tell the facts," claiming it would destroy him; so instead, in a public letter to a friend who had asked him why he did not reply to the rumors and charges circulated by Mrs. Woodhull, Tilton wrote:

> . . . when the truth is a sword, God's mercy sometimes commands it sheathed. If you think I do not burn to defend my wife and little ones, you know not the fiery spirit within me . . . But my wife's heart is more a fountain of charity, and quenches all resentments . . . From the beginning, she has stood with her hand on my lips,

saying 'Hush!' So . . . I shall try with patience to keep
my anger within my own breast, lest it shoot forth like
a thunderbolt through other hearts.

This scarcely helped matters, and both Beecher and
Moulton reprimanded Tilton for having only made the
scandal hotter. As knowledge of it spread, the deacons of
Plymouth Church tried vainly to stave off outside ecclesiastic intervention by restoring harmony within. When, a year
before, Tilton had arbitrated his broken contract with Henry
Bowen, the publisher, for $7,000, a simultaneous "Tri-Partite
Covenant" had secretly been signed by Bowen, Tilton, and
Beecher. Bowen had promised to stop indulging in his chronic
whisperings about Beecher's past adulteries and had declared
he knew "nothing derogatory to his reputation as a clergyman or a man." Tilton had renewed his faith in the pastor as
"a grandly good and generous man," and Beecher had said
it was "a joy" to resume his old relations of "love, respect
and alliance" with both men and had promised to repair any
damage he had done to "their standing and fame as Christian
gentlemen." A friend of Beecher's, Sam Wilkeson, who was a
prominent member of the church and a well-known journalist
on the *Tribune*, now published the covenant, hoping it would
silence the scandalmongers. Tilton was furious. He claimed
it made him out to be the chief apologist, and he threatened
to retaliate by publishing Beecher's much earlier "Letter of
Contrition," in which Beecher, through Moulton, had said:
"I humble myself before him as I do before my God."

Beecher had a fresh fit of resignation and wrote to Moulton,
for publication, an announcement that he was quitting because
he could no longer "save from shame a certain household."
Tilton was even more furious. He told Moulton: "You may tell
Mr. Beecher, if he resigns his ministry in this crisis, flinging
back that shadow on my family I will shoot him on the street."
In Tilton's mood, it was no idle threat. Beecher withdrew his
resignation offer, but soon dangled it again, in a fit of inner
surrender. He wrote Moulton:

MUSIC TO HIS EARS

*Beecher listens to applause for him during a prayer meeting conducted
in Plymouth Church by his assistant.*

MY DEAR FRANK: The whole earth is tranquil and the heaven is serene, as befits one who has about finished his world-life . . . I have determined to make no more resistance. Theodore's temperament is such that the future, even if temporarily earned, would be absolutely worthless, filled with abrupt charges, and rendering me liable at any hour or day to be obliged to stultify all the devices by which we have saved ourselves . . . My mind is clear. I shall write for the public a statement that will bear the light of the judgment day. God will take care of me and mine. When I look on earth it is a deep night. When I look to the heavens above I see the morning breaking. But, Oh, that I could put in golden letters my deep sense of your faithful, earnest, undying fidelity, your disinterested friendship. Your noble wife, too, has been to me one of God's comforters . . . There is no use in further trying. I have a strong feeling upon me, and it brings great peace with it, that I am spending my *last Sunday* and preaching my last sermon. Dear, good God, I thank thee I am indeed beginning to see rest and triumph. The pain of life is but a moment; the glory of everlasting emancipation is wordless, inconceivable. Oh, my beloved Frank, I shall know you there, and forever hold fellowship with you, and look back and smile at the past.

Your loving
H. W. B.

Beecher would regret his kind words about Moulton and his wife, but for the moment they were the only friends he could turn to; ultimately, Emma Moulton's accounts of conversations with him would bound back to his disadvantage even more sharply than Moulton's. In the absence of that safer instrument, the telephone, the written record would substantiate the Moultons' joint patience and solicitude. As soon as he received Beecher's letter, Moulton sat down and answered it:

MY DEAR FRIEND: Your letter makes this first Sabbath of Summer dark and cold like a vault. You have never inspired me with courage or hope, and if I had listened to you alone my hands would have dropped helpless long ago. You don't begin to be in the danger today that has faced you many times before. If you now look it square in the eyes, it will cower and shrink away again. You know that I have never been in sympathy with, but that I absolutely abhor, the unmanly mood out of which your letter of this morning came. This mood is a reservoir of mildew. *You* can stand if the *whole case* were published tomorrow. In my opinion it shows only a selfish faith in God to go whining into heaven, if you could, with a truth that you are not courageous enough, with God's help and a faith in God, to try to live on earth. You know that I love you, and because I do I shall try and try as in the past. . .

As a self-styled "heathen," Moulton was surely making good on his earlier promise to the pastor to do what he could. Much would later be made of the phrase "*You* can stand if the *whole case* were published tomorrow," but the theory that this indicated Moulton's belief in Beecher's innocence was thoroughly contradicted by everything else Moulton and his wife said and did in their valiant but vain attempt to protect both Beecher and Tilton and keep the scandal hushed.

The desperation of the quashers had now, however, reached new heights. With Beecher's permission, some friends of his in Plymouth Church who had heard facts or rumors about the affair tried to induce Tilton to go abroad with his family, and more than hints were dropped that all expenses would be paid. But this fell through as quickly as the recommendations Tilton had made that Beecher take a trip to Palestine. Beecher's mood fell so low that when Moulton begged him, Tilton took pity on the pastor and, in a rare gesture recalling their earlier affection, slipped a note onto his pulpit one Sunday morning: "Grace, mercy, peace," signing his initials, "T. T." A day or two later Beecher told Tilton that there had "never been a sunbeam" that had brought him more lightness than that.

At length, to try to pacify Tilton as persuaded by the Moultons, Beecher sent two letters to the *Brooklyn Eagle.* In the first he denied Tilton had been the author of any "calumnies" against him, and said that if the publication of the earlier "Tri-Partite Covenant" had so implied, "it will do him a great injustice." In the second the preacher finally declared what his friends had been demanding of him. He wrote:

> I have seen in the morning papers that application has been made to Mrs. Victoria Woodhull for certain letters of mine supposed to contain information respecting certain infamous stories against me. She has two business letters, one declining an invitation to a suffrage meeting, and the other declining to give the assistance solicited. These and all letters of mine in the hands of any other persons, they have my cordial consent to publish. I will only add, in this connection, that the stories and rumors which have, for a time, been circulated about me, are grossly untrue, and I stamp them, in general and in particular, as utterly false.

There remained something mysterious about the timing of this letter. The "application" to Mrs. Woodhull that Beecher spoke about had been made by none other than Henry Bowen, who, after the "Tri-Partite Covenant" had been let out, considered his own lips unsealed. Things having gone as far as they had, Bowen once more had changed his tack. His earlier betrayal of Theodore Tilton in the effort to drive Beecher, as the man who had cuckolded them both, out of Brooklyn now seemed a mistake. But Bowen, as always, moved cautiously. He went to see "The Woodhull," taking the exaggerated precaution of dragging eleven friends and relatives along. Mrs. Woodhull had let drop some remarks that she possessed certain letters that could "sink Beecher 40,000 fathoms deep." Bowen wanted to know how incriminating her evidence was. "I informed him

[Bowen] that I proposed to keep the purport of those letters to myself," Victoria Woodhull subsequently told a reporter. The letters remained a mystery, even after they came up again, dramatically, at the court trial. There were many who did not feel Mrs. Woodhull had manufactured them, ectoplasmically. They suspected that Henry Ward Beecher's friends had seen to it that they were safely returned to him, for a price, before the preacher wrote that long-delayed letter to the *Eagle*.

It was, at any rate, a little late. Some members of Plymouth Church, led by William West, a former deacon, feeling that "the only way to meet the scandal was to strike it down and utterly destroy it," moved to expel Tilton for his association with Mrs. Woodhull and for slandering Beecher. Beecher did his best to hold them off. It was "not a good time to bring this matter before the church," he said, but Brother West, whom some called "a pious Paul Pry," was adamant, being moved, he said, "by a sense of duty." It became apparent that West was trying to smoke Beecher out too, even when the pastor became "angry and threatening." West had talked, among others, to Martha Bradshaw, the deaconess whom Tilton had first consulted about his wife's adultery confession back in the hot summer of 1870. In desperation, Mrs. Bradshaw had now begged Beecher to say he was innocent of the charge. "Do mitigate it, be it so ever little, if you can," she wrote him. He replied: "I think you will do the greatest good to all parties by pursuing the course which I have done from the first, namely, refusing to allow the public to meddle with domestic and private affairs." There was no longer any doubt in poor Mrs. Bradshaw's mind.

Beecher's public denial, however, was widely welcomed. The *Eagle* praised him "as one of the few who shed on Brooklyn a lustre that advances her fame throughout the world." Prominent persons were interviewed in the Brooklyn Club and in Faust's. "Inspector Folk, who never speaks much on any subject, declared, after reading the letter, that Beecher was a brick," was a typical response. But elsewhere there were growing doubts about the pastor of Plymouth Church. The *Chicago Times* commented that "for years the sword of Damocles has been suspended above his platform," and added: "Come to the front and center, Henry Ward Beecher, you are but human—let us have the truth though the heavens fall!" "It's a disgusting mess, all of it," said the *Hartford Times*. "It shows the practical fruits of 'free love-ism.'" The *Mercury Mail*, in Middletown, N. Y., spoke for thousands of hinterland and rural folk when it decried "this vial of scandal whose odors the world today is snuffing up its nostrils." Even in Brooklyn there appeared an opposition press. The *Sunday Press* took a long summary look at Plymouth Church, at "the jaded merchant and the languishing belle" who repaired there "twice a week for the stimulation of their devotional senses and the perfuming of their moral characters," who let Beecher's "unctuous syllables drop, like overrunning incense, on their creamy overcoats," and added

"EXTRA! EXTRA!" NEWSBOYS HAWKING A SCANDAL BREAK

a few special barbs at "the simpering misses who preface their Sunday flirtations with a flood of easy tears, while he launders and lightnings and sheds a soft spiritual rain from his flowery platform." The *Press* pulled no punches and included Henry Bowen in its broadsides, describing him as "one who has combined the greed of a Shylock with the treachery of a Judas Iscariot." Beecher, the paper roared, "hugs to his breast the two men who have pronounced him the ravisher of their relatives, while they, self-proclaimed cowards, allied to each other only by their common infamy, set down in writing their promise never to allude to his crimes again. Verily a sweet-savored trio this . . ." If the breaking-open of the scandal did nothing else, it was beginning surely to clear the air—which was really all Victoria Woodhull had wanted.

It remained for a young journalist in Troy, N. Y., to drive the point home most clearly—that the time had come for some solid, sensible thinking, free of false pride, false loyalties, and fancy moralizing. His name was Edward H. G. Clark, of the *Troy Whig* and the *Troy Daily Press*. Raised in the Abolitionist tradition of William Lloyd Garrison, and a friend of Tilton's accordingly, he became interested in the case through Tilton, but he spared no one in a handsomely printed four-page leaflet he called the *Thunderbolt*, taking his title from Tilton's phrase. In its panoplied headline the *Thunderbolt* declared:

The Republic Threatened!
The Beecher-Tilton Scandal
and the
Beecher-Bowen-Comstock Conspiracy.
The Seal Broken at Last.
Woodhull's "Lies" and Theodore Tilton's "True Story."
The Account Horrible at Best,
No "Obscenity" but God's Truth.
The Sexual Ethics of Plymouth Church—a New
Revelation—
The Brooklyn Saints
Torture Saint Paul Into a Free Lover.

The Thunderbolt Shatters a Bad Crowd and Plows Up The Whole Ground.

Clark printed Tilton's so-called "True Story," with careful checking, and he ended by calling Tilton "a wretch" for his own brand of moral cowardice and wishy-washy romanticism. Mrs. Woodhull, Clark said, "ought to be hanged," but she also "ought to have a monument erected to her memory at the foot of the gallows." *Woodhull and Claflin's Weekly* sounds like "the gabblings of a frog pond," he added, "yet the amazing journal is crowded with thought and with needed information that can be got nowhere else." Beecher fared worse than the other principals in the case. But Clark's chief aim was to strike a blow for the freedom of the press. "That holy horror should gripe the bowels of the whole New York press at the two-penny corruptions of Woodhull and Claflin is enough to make the mummy of Bennett wink with its cock-eye," he cried.

All this publicity had its inevitable effect. In October 1873, though there was no evidence that he had slandered Beecher, Tilton was formally read out of Plymouth Church by a 210-to-13 vote. He confronted Beecher at a public meeting. "If the minister of this church has anything whereof to accuse me, let him now speak and I shall answer as God is my judge," he said. Beecher stood up amid a vast silence, broken only by the sobbing of women in their handkerchiefs. He had no charge, the pastor said. "Whatever differences have been between us have been amicably adjusted." There was great applause, but it sounded hollow to Beecher, who still feared the worst. It soon happened. Dr. Storrs, Beecher's former friend and fellow pastor, whom Tilton had again consulted, now claimed that Plymouth Church had acted contrary to church law. "Let us maintain the purity of Congregational policy," he cried, even when pastoral friends were concerned. Beecher was furious. Storrs was simply jealous, he said, and the interference was "an unspeakable outrage." He wrote to Frank Moulton: "I am in hopes that

Theodore, who has borne so much, will be unwilling to be a flail in Storrs' hand to strike a friend. He [Storrs] is determined to force a conflict and to use one of us to destroy the other . . . *It ought to damn Storrs!*"

Storrs proved not the only leading Congregationalist who disapproved of the way Beecher had handled the dismissal of Theodore Tilton. Over the protests of Plymouth Church, the ecclesiastic wheels were soon set in motion for an Advisory Council to be called. Under Congregational policy, there is no Presbytery, Synod, General Assembly, Diocese, House of Bishops, or any other body that rules member churches, but if it is felt that any one church has violated generally accepted Congregational doctrine or procedure, a council can be mustered to consider the issue. In the case of Tilton's dismissal, it was held that church law had been violated because he had not severed his connection with Plymouth Church by voluntarily writing a letter to another church, or because he had not been summoned before a church tribunal.

Beecher, who had always been one of the most independent members of the loose federation of Congregational churches, refused at once to subject himself or his church to any council judgement. "We can whisk the Council down the wind," he cried. "We can set them all agog!" He would not appear before it, he insisted. "I won't! I won't!" he said. "I say to them that gave me these words of cruelty and wrong, 'God will smite thee, thou whited wall!'"—but leading Congregationaists trekked to Brooklyn from all over the country and the sessions, held at the Clinton Avenue Church in Brooklyn, began.

Bravely, Beecher went ahead with his annual pew-sale. A story in the *Brooklyn Union* described it as "Beecher's Auction." The wealthy Heights parishioners arrived with pencils and diagrams, it said, "and with a little more boisterousness one might have imagined himself at a horse sale, in which a Derby winner was the first choice." A total of $59,430 was raised, which was $129 more than the previous year, and the *New York Commercial Advertiser* figured out that "despite the

Beecher-Tilton imbroglio, and the recent independent movement of the church, Mr. Beecher had advanced in the estimation of his congregation a little more than one-quarter of one
percent." Beecher was manic. "Well, it's going better than I
expected," he told another reporter. "What do you think of
these for panic prices!"

When the Council, despite Plymouth Church's snubbing
of it, only slapped the church on the wrist without disfellow-
shipping it for the way in which it had handled the Tilton case,
Beecher breathed still easier. He rushed off to Twin Mountain
House in New Hampshire, where he played croquet with fresh
zest. A correspondent for the *World* followed him up and wrote:
"To see him rushing from wicket to post, dropping on his knees
to sight the shots, rejoicing over the discomfiture of his adver-
saries, and driving his ball along to victory was a revelation of
what can be done when the man and the mallet come together."
Back in Brooklyn, the *New York Herald* called the Council
"an attempt to take revenge on a brother minister because the
Almighty made him a genius," and the *New York Tribune*, even
more harshly, told the Council members, "Go home, gentlemen, and let your betters alone. Quarrel with each other, if you
must, but do not wear your knuckles to the bone in hitting a
giant. Gentlemen, find your gingham umbrellas, and go home."

The case might have died there had not Beecher's friends
pushed it. Thomas ("Tearful Tommy") Shearman, a prominent
lawyer who was an intimate defender of the peculative Jim Fisk
in Manhattan and was also the clerk of Plymouth Church,
called Tilton "out of his mind" and blamed Mrs. Tilton for telling "incredible stories" about her pastor in "mediumistic fits."
Shearman, later one of Beecher's trial attorneys, apologized,
but the preacher was in a funk. "Is there no end of trouble?"
he wrote Moulton. "My innermost soul longs for peace, and if
that cannot be, for death—that *will* bring *peace*."

Even worse, a prominent theologian, Dr. Leonard Bacon, of
Yale, who had been Moderator of the Council, wrote six articles
and lectured about the ecclesiastic aspects of the case at the Yale
Divinity School. Plymouth Church, he said, "had thrown away

BEECHER AT PLAY

The pastor enjoys croquet in the mountains.

the opportunity of vindicating its pastor," and "Mr. Beecher would have done better to have let vengeance come on the heads of his slanderers." He alluded to Tilton as "a knave" and "a dog," and Tilton at last blew up and performed the final act that forced Beecher to counterattack. He wrote a long public reply to Dr. Bacon, setting forth all the facts of the case, noting the tendency "to sacrifice *my* good name for the sake of *his*"—Beecher's—and ending by publishing, for the first time, the highly incriminating, humble apology Beecher had written him through Frank Moulton three and a half years before.

CHAPTER XI

There was only one thing left for Beecher to do—air the scandal by staging a trial in his own church. The autonomy granted each of the Congregational churches to conduct its own affairs was an ample one, and Beecher appointed a committee of six members of Plymouth Church to look into what he termed "the rumors, insinuations, or charges respecting my conduct." No ecclesiastic doctrine was involved here, and the fact that he singlehandedly picked his own jury, which chose its own examiners from among prominent attorneys who were both loyal parishioners and Beecher's close friends, seemed scarcely to arouse other Congregationalists any more than it disturbed the generally idolatrous public; if it did, the ministers remained silent, for the moment anyway. After the trials of Henry Ward Beecher, both ecclesiastic and civil, had occupied the country's attention for two years steadily, there were critics both in and out of the church who were more ready to express their disapproval of Beecher's private form of obtaining "justice."

Even now, however, in the summer of 1874, there were frantic last-minute efforts at compromise. Frank Moulton tried to get Beecher to resign quietly, without having to admit any wrong, but the pastor had changed his mind and seemed suddenly more intent on brazening things through, especially after both Shearman and Benjamin Tracy, another lawyer and prominent Republican who was advising Beecher, convinced him that Tilton and Moulton were blackmailers because of the money he had voluntarily given them to help Tilton's *Golden Age*. Beecher was skeptical about the blackmail charge, but he went along with his defenders, who were willing by now to try anything to save the preacher, his church, and their bonds. Tracy also tried once more to get Tilton to quit the country with his family and go to Europe, but Tilton was as adamant as Beecher in preferring a showdown.

At the last second Beecher had a flash of nobility. When his lecture agent, James Redpath, relayed the information that Tilton was going to make the open charge of adultery instead of "unhandsome advances" toward Elizabeth Tilton, Beecher told him: "I shall make a clean breast of it, I shall tell the whole truth, I shall take the blame on myself." But he did not, nor did he hold his over-eager supporters in check.

BUT SCANDAL WILL OUT

Strange that a difference there   *"You ain't done nothin'," says Parson B.*
should be 'Twixt Tweedledum and   *"The same to you!" says Theodore T.*
Tweedledee!

Secretly, it was arranged for Elizabeth Tilton to leave her husband and flee to friends the morning after she was coached on her testimony to the church committee and was ready to appear in Beecher's behalf. "I rose quietly," she said later, "and, having dressed, roused him only to say, 'Theodore, I will never take another step by your side. The end has indeed come.'" Lib Tilton was now a cog in the grinding machinery set up to defend her pastor, who was scarcely to reciprocate by defending her any further in the heat of the crusade to vindicate himself. "I think for the sake of Mr. Beecher, for the sake of his influence on the world, for my position, for my children, it is my duty to deny it," she said of her adultery in explaining her actions to a friend. "You will always find the adulteress with the adulterer," was to be the clipped reply of Tilton's lawyer. Elizabeth Tilton's worst ordeal was still to come, when, years later, she would no longer be able to face the lie she was about to live with publicly, but in helping to furnish the flimsy foundations of Henry Ward Beecher's defense, she was now to sustain countless others in their belief that even if he acted foolishly, the preacher of Plymouth Church was still the greatest man in America.

As she did not appear in court as a witness, what she told the committee was the only testimony she gave in the case. She was the first person summoned and immediately declared she had never been guilty of adultery with Henry Ward Beecher "in thought, or deed, nor has he ever offered me an indecorous or improper proposal." Tilton, she said, was madly jealous, "the God of battles was in him, as demonstrated by his heartless attempt "to convince the world that I am or ever have been unable to distinguish between an innocent or a guilty love." Her husband, she continued, "lived to crush Mr. Beecher . . . his hatred has existed these many years." She said: "I owe to my friendship with Mr. Beecher, as to no other human instrumentality, that encouragement in my mental life, and that growth toward the divine nature, which enable me to walk daily in the lively hope of the life beyond . . . The implication that the harmony of the house was unbroken 'til Mr. Beecher entered it as a frequent guest and friend is a lamentable satire upon the household where he [Tilton] himself, years before, laid the cornerstone of free love and desecrated its altars up to the time of my departure, so that the atmosphere was not only godless but impure for my children. And in this effort and throe of agony, I would fain lift my daughters, and all womanhood, from the insidious and diabolical teachings of these latter days."

As for her confession, Mrs. Tilton had this explanation. Her husband, she said, had accused her of having "a sensual influence over men" and his way was so great that "a mesmeric condition was brought to bear upon me," which resulted in her having written the letter that Beecher had propositioned her. "I was pretty nearly out of my mind, and my attitude was that I shan't be here very long anyway, so if you want me to do this, I will do it . . . I knew there was trouble and I thought it would some way serve Theodore and bring peace to his household." The confession, she claimed, only concerned her need for other emotional outlets. "I do not think if I had known as much as I do now of Tilton I should ever have encouraged Mr. Beecher's acquaintance," she declared. "I think I did wrong in doing it, inasmuch as it hurt Theodore." But, she went on, "There was always a damper between Theodore and me, but there never was between me and Mr. Beecher. I often said, 'Theodore, if you had given me what you give to others, I dare say I would find in you what I find in Mr. Beecher. He appreciated me. With Mr. Beecher I had a sort of consciousness of being more. I felt myself another woman." A committee member interrupted to ask: "You mean he gave you self-respect?" Mrs. Tilton replied: "Yes, I never felt a bit of embarrassment with Mr. Beecher, but to this day I never could sit down with Theodore without being self-conscious and feeling his sense of my inequality with him."

The subject of the Tilton's home life was to furnish editorialists henceforth with ample material. *Leslie's Illustrated Newspaper*, for example, took note of Tilton's declaration that he would give five hundred dollars if his wife were three inches taller and commented that "She was too exacting with a man who was earning his bread in the treadmill of the daily press . . . It was plain she had touches of genius, and yet lived under the broad cloak of the commonplace . . . His pining for a tall woman [was] a sort of generous Oriental disposition to value the female physique at the rate of $160 and some odd cents a lineal inch. He dreamed of a woman possessing great physical and mental charms, a woman like Woodhull, with the mind of a Demosthenes . . . so he rushed madly into the clouds and plucked down for his domestic gallery a debauched Psyche. There was nothing congenial between Tilton and his wife. Even when they talked gushingly there was a meaningless strain of the imagination."

Great efforts had been made by Beecher's friends to persuade Tilton not to tell the committee the whole truth, to get him still to admit some grievance less than adultery, to "spare this old man the blow you are about to strike him," as one of them put it; but Tilton by this time was irreconcilable. He immediately charged Beecher with "criminal seduction" and "a crime of uncommon wrongfulness and perfidy." In tracing the long history of the case, he gave the play-by-play story of his wife's confession, her retraction at Beecher's frantic dictation, and then her recantation of the retraction—all of which had weirdly taken place that same December night in 1870—and also referred to Beecher's frequent allusions to guilt in statements and letters that had followed.

The clandestine courtship between Elizabeth and her pastor went back a long time, Tilton said. He spoke of having years ago witnessed "an improper caress" of Mrs. Tilton on Beecher's part when "very slyly" he touched "her ankles and her lower limbs" as they were looking at some engravings on the library floor, and of having on another occasion entered the room unexpectantly to find Mrs. Tilton standing, abashed, and Beecher "in an ottoman chair, with his vest unbuttoned and his face colored like a rose." He had accepted her explanation that she wanted to have "a quiet talk" with Beecher and had locked the door to keep the children out, Tilton said, but after her confession the episode became part of a reconstructed pattern and made him realize that Beecher had slowly "ensnared her." Mrs. Tilton "could only have been swerved from the path of

THE CHURCH HEARING

*Tilton charges Beecher with adultery before the Plymouth
Church investigating committee.*

rectitude by artful and powerful persuasions, clothed in the phrases of religion," he added. "If Mr. Beecher held the same religious views I did, he never could have made any approach to her. I do not believe in point of moral goodness, barring some drawbacks, that there is in this company so white a soul as Elizabeth Tilton," but "for such a large moral nature, there is a lack of certain balance and equipoise." She was always "in a sort of vaporous cloud, between light and dark," said Tilton.

The committee tried hard to counteract what he described as "the desolation of my heart and life" by bringing up his own alleged acts of adultery and attentions to other women; but in spite of what his wife had said, his clerical cross-examiners were unable to get very far. Attempts to portray Tilton as overly familiar with some of his suffragist friends particularly failed. He admitted he played chess with Elizabeth Cady Stanton late in the evening at his house sometimes, but when asked if he had ever appeared in her guest-room or in Susan Anthony's before they were dressed, he replied: "No, and I cannot imagine any reasons why anyone should."

The following exchange between Tilton and Benjamin Tracy, an attorney and prominent political leader, was typical of the committee's attitude:

> TRACY: Don't you know that your wife's mind has been disturbed in regard to your own infidelity to her by your associations with public women?
> TILTON: I have never associated with public women.
> TRACY: I don't mean prostitutes, I mean reformers.
> TILTON: Oh, yes . . . Elizabeth had been annoyed by my association with all persons out of the realm of religious and orthodox ideas.

Although the proceedings before the committee were supposed to be secret, the testimony kept leaking out in one newspaper or another. The *Brooklyn Argus* published Tilton's statement the day after he made it, whereupon the committee decided to make public his cross-examination. When it was all out, *Leslie's* commented: "We are reading the most marvelous of human dramas, greater in plot, development and effect than Hawthorne's 'The Scarlet Letter,' Charles Reade's 'Griffith Gaunt,' George Eliot's 'Romola,' or Shakespeare's 'Othello.' It has its only counterpart in 'Faust.'"

Two days after the *Argus* publication, Beecher made a statement to the press. For the time being, he still defended Elizabeth Tilton. "One less deserving of such disgrace I never knew," he said. "I cherish for her a pure feeling, such as a gentleman might honorably offer to a Christian woman, and which he might receive and reciprocate without moral scruple . . . Even to be suspected of having offered, under the privileges of a peculiarly sacred relation, an indecorum to a wife and mother, could not but deeply wound anyone who is sensitive to the honor of womanhood." The preacher did not appear before the committee until near the end of the "trial." In the meantime, the third major figure, Frank Moulton, did. Efforts had been made, first

REPORTERS INTERVIEW TILTON

through Beecher himself and then secretly through the pastor's friends, to get Moulton to return some of the vital letters in the case. Tilton was even offered a large sum to "release" Moulton from his promise to keep all the documents in the case "in trust" for the protection of both principals. Moulton stuck to his guns. He refused to surrender part of the papers, and then told the committee, almost pleading with them, that it would be best for everyone concerned if all the letters remained secret. Had it not been for Beecher's committee performance following Moulton's plea, and for the whitewash the committee applied, Moulton would have kept silent.

During the early part of the committee's sessions, Beecher had made a point of staying on his farm in Peekskill. Here, with his friend and lawyer, Shearman, he mapped out his statement. Late in July the *Herald* sent a reporter up to describe the pastoral setting. "At an early hour the great preacher is astir," the account read. "The dew still lies heavy upon the greensward as he strolls leisurely through the spacious grounds. Mr. Beecher looks poorly. The lines are deeper drawn, and there are traces of suffering and care upon his countenance. There is placidity of old, but it is the placidity of repression, the crowding back of a sorrow that will not down. Plainly, Mr. Beecher cannot say with Paul, 'None of these things move me.' He moves mechanically, as though preoccupied, and only when some strikingly beautiful object in flower or shrub meets his eye do his features light up with the old-time animation."

Two weeks later, Beecher appeared in Brooklyn to make his official explanation to his privately picked church jury. He was determined by now, it soon became clear, to save himself at the expense of anyone, even Elizabeth Tilton. He now spoke of her "excessive affection for me" and said it had been unsought. In hurt tones he referred to her secret confession of alleged adultery to her husband, a fortnight after she had solicited the advice of both Mrs. Beecher and himself about a separation, as "communicating a very needless treachery to her friend and pastor." (Elizabeth Cady Stanton was to exclaim, when she read this: "With what withering cruelty his words must have fallen

BEECHER AT HIS FARM IN PEEKSKILL

on her heart.") The preacher then spoke of his visits to Mrs. Tilton, of his frolicking with the children and of being treated as one of the family. "At no interview which ever took place," he said, "did anything occur which might not have occurred with perfect propriety between a brother and a sister, between a father and a child." Admitting that "by blind heedlessness and friendship" he had perhaps "beguiled her heart," Beecher now explained the extravagance of his repentance by declaring: "The great interests which were entirely dependent upon me, the church which I had built up, the book which I was writing, my own immediate family, my brother's name, now engaged in the ministry, my sisters, the name which I had hoped might live after me and be in some slight degree a source of strength and encouragement to those who should succeed me, and above all the cause for which I had devoted my life, seemed imperiled.

It seemed to me that my life work was to end abruptly . . . and in disaster."

As for what he had written of resigning, or killing himself, or of fleeing abroad to avoid public exposure, some details of which Tilton had also referred to, the pastor had this explanation: "I am one upon whom trouble works inwardly, making me outwardly silent, but reverberating in the chambers of my soul; and when at length I do speak it is a pent-up flood, and pours without measure or moderation. I inherit a tendency to sadness, the remains in me of a positive hypochondria in my father and grandfather, and in certain moods of reaction the world becomes black and I see very despairingly . . . This manifestation is in such contrast to the hopefulness and courage which I experience in ordinary times that none but those intimate with me would suspect one so full of overflowing spirit and eager gladsomeness to have within him a care of gloom and despondency. . ."

Knowing he would not have this opportunity for sentimental introspection in any court, Beecher took full advantage of the freedom of expression he still had in his pastoral precincts. At his eloquent best after he received a bouquet from a group of female parishioners, he spared neither Tilton, now his open antagonist, nor Moulton, the friend the preacher had unfortunately admitted, in writing, had been "sent by God." Tilton, the preacher said, "I can see now . . . is and has been from the beginning of this difficulty a reckless schemer, pursuing a plan of mingled greed and hatred, and weaving about me a network of suspicions, misunderstandings, plots and lies, to which my own innocent words and acts—nay, even my thoughts of kindness toward him—have been made to contribute." Beecher had previously admitted his share of responsibility for the dismissal of Tilton from the editorship of the *Independent* and from the *Brooklyn Union* editor's chair. Penitent, after Moulton's intervention, he now referred to his having "naively" helped finance the *Golden Age* for Tilton to edit.

Tilton's "perpetual follies and blunders rendered his recovery impossible," the preacher said. Then he spoke disparagingly of what he himself had condoned, the mollification of Victoria Woodhull before she broke the scandal story. "To restore to popularity and public confidence one who in the midst of my efforts in his behalf patronized disreputable people and doctrines" proved too much, he said of Tilton. "It was hard to do anything for such a man. I might as well have tried to fill a sieve with water." He denied vehemently what Mrs. Woodhull had said, that he was himself "a free lover" in theory as well as in practice. "I am not versed in the casuistry of free love," the pastor declared. "The circle of which Mrs. Woodhull formed a part was the center of loathsome scandals, organized, classified and perpetuated with a greedy and unclean appetite for everything that was foul and vile . . . I appeal to you and to all Christian men to judge whether almost any personal sacrifice ought not to have been made rather than to suffer the morals of an entire community, especially of the young, to be corrupted by the filthy details of scandalous falsehoods." He referred, finally, to the scandal as "an open pool of corruption exhaling

A MYSTERIOUS WITNESS ELUDES THE REPORTERS

deadly vapors." The nation had done nothing but listen to it for six weeks, he said, and that should be enough. "Not a great war nor a revolution could have more filled the newspapers than this question of domestic trouble, magnified a thousand-fold, and, like a sore spot on the human body, drawing to itself every morbid humor in the blood. Whoever is buried with it, it is time that this abomination be buried below all touch or power of resurrection."

This was, of course, what Beecher would have wished; but his statement received more press attention than the impeachment attempt against President Johnson. Thirty Associated Press men alone covered it. The gauntlet having been thrown down, Theodore Tilton lost no time in picking it up. On August 20, 1874, even before the church committee issued its report, he swore out his complaint in City Court against Beecher, charging the sixty-one-year-old pastor with having willfully alienated and destroyed Mrs. Tilton's affections for her husband, and demanding $100,000 for his having "wholly lost the comfort, society, aid and assistance of his said wife." Beecher was up in the White Mountains, where he went each summer for his hay fever, and he did not even return to Brooklyn a fortnight later when his chosen clerical defenders cleared him. Their absolution was just what might have been expected. In a public pronouncement, handed down like an ordinary court decision, they declared him the victim of Tilton's "malicious and revengeful designs." Elizabeth Tilton's conduct was called "indefensible" because she had given vent to her "inordinate affection." Absolving the preacher of any "unchaste or improper act," the committee found "nothing whatever in the evidence that should impair the perfect confidence of Plymouth Church or the world in the Christian character or integrity of Henry Ward Beecher." As a favorite child might be reprimanded, he was censured only for having allowed his abounding generosity and love to blind him and lead him to drop his guard with the Tiltons.

The Examining Committee of Plymouth Church, a standing body in contrast to the special committee Beecher had appointed, formally received the report and promptly under-lined the decision by calling Tilton and Moulton guilty of "the most infamous conspiracy known to the present age." At a packed meeting of the whole church, one of its leading mem-bers, a professional elocutionist, Professor Robert Raymond, read the summary aloud. Applause was "uncontrollable" and extended to Pineapple Street outside, where an overflow crowd heard snatches through the open doors. In the midst of the proceedings Frank Moulton suddenly appeared through a side door and took a seat in front. The tension was instantaneous. When Professor Raymond interpolated a remark of his own, that "Moulton has poisoned the minds of the public with his infernal lies," Moulton jumped up and shouted: "You are a liar, sir." Men in the audience rushed forward, some of them brandishing pistols, and, according to one account, "struggled to get at Moulton, with the intention of chastising him." "Put him out, put him out!" the crowd shouted. "You can't do it, sir," Moulton said to a man alongside him. The police helped restore order, and the final resolutions were read, supporting Beecher's "entire innocence and purity" and declaring "that our confi-dence in and love for our pastor, so far from being diminished, is heightened and deepened by the unmerited suffering he has so long borne, and we welcome him with a sympathy more tender and a trust more unbounded than we ever did before to his public labors among us, to our church, our families, our homes, our hearts." Three thousand voices shouted "Aye!" and only one, Moulton's, said "Nay." Since he was not a member of the congregation, his vote was not counted. The audience started singing "Praise God from whom all blessings flow" as the meeting ended. On the way out Moulton had to be pro-tected by two policemen, who put him into a carriage as the crowd stood by and cried "Iago."

The nation-wide reaction by now was almost as intense and emotional as that of the partisans of Plymouth Church. Led by the metropolitan press, most of the East was for Beecher, even when Moulton and Tilton revealed more facts of the vain conspiracy to hush and lessen the scandal and further

TEMPERS FLARE IN CHURCH

Professor Raymond, announcing the acquittal of Beecher by the Plymouth Church committee. Moulton promptly calls him "a liar."

documented the preacher's countless expressions of guilt. The preacher's attorneys declared: "Better were it for the inhabitants of this city that every brick and every stone in its buildings were swallowed by an earthquake, or melted by fire, than that its brightest ornament, its most honored name, should sink into deep infamy." But the fact that the deacons of the church had gone to such sophistic extremes to clear Beecher was beginning to arouse resentment elsewhere, and what Moulton said, in backing up the detailed evidence he now no longer shrank from publicizing, was more and more damaging. The pastor had told him, Moulton claimed, that "My acts of intercourse

THE ATTACK ON MOULTON

Scene in vestibule of Plymouth Church as friends of Beecher berate Moulton for opposing the preacher's exculpation by a church "jury."

with that woman were as natural and sincere an expression of my love for her as the words of endearment which I addressed to her" and were "so pure" that the little red lounge in the Tilton, home on Livingston Street was "almost a sacred thing." Tilton made another long statement, too, in which he said that he had forgiven his wife "because I tenderly remembered that Christ Himself forgave a similar fault in a more wicked woman," but of Beecher he added: "In contemplating my empty house, my scattered children, and my broken home, I thank heaven that my heart is spared the pangs of this man's remorse for having wrought a ruin which not even Almighty God can repair."

Moulton, when he had made public, reluctantly, the letters in the case, including the clandestine ones Beecher and Elizabeth Tilton had exchanged, had made special mention of Mrs. Tilton's note of May 3, 1871, in which she had referred to her "weapons" as "love, a large untiring generosity, and nest-hiding." What, exactly, Moulton asked, is nest-hiding? He called on Beecher to explain the term "in his first sermon after his vacation." Beecher remained silent on the subject until he came into court, but one of his over-zealous supporters rushed in with a definition. Professor Raymond, Moulton's antagonist in church, wrote a letter to the *Eagle*. "Whatever nest-hiding is," he said, "it is evidently a means used by Mrs. Tilton *at home* and one by which she sought to bear her suffering alone, and to keep Mr. Beecher forever ignorant of it." Professor Raymond then gave his own example of what he thought the preacher had meant. Three years earlier, he said, he had taken a party of friends out to Yellowstone Park, and one evening they had shot at the head of an eagle, poking up out of its nest in a cottonwood tree. The next day they had gone to the tree, and found the mother eagle dead in the nest, with her eaglets still alive and protected beneath her. "She had taken her death-wounds in silence, and covered her young to the last," said Professor Raymond. "That was *nest-hiding*, and that was what Mrs. Tilton tried to do, using love, forgiveness and secrecy concerning the wounds which were daily inflicted upon her." Tilton, the professor said, had been guilty of "nest-fouling."

As other secrets of the case rolled forth, newspapers had a field day unraveling them. Every last detail was gone into, and every possible source of information sought out. Grocers, butchers, shoemakers who had serviced the Tiltons or the Beechers were interviewed. Beecher's tiniest response was noted, the state of his digestion and respiratory condition, how he welcomed a group of faithful followers at his Peekskill farm on Sunday. It was duly reported that on the same day Tilton drove with a friend to Engeman's Ocean House at Coney Island, and that "after a stroll on the beach, the gentlemen dined on clams and bluefish, and, returning, reached the city at nine o'clock." The protagonists' homes in Brooklyn became regular beats. "The reporter on duty at the top of the tree opposite Moulton's house has his food passed up to him through a section of garden-hose," a columnist wrote. A reporter who visited Tilton's place on Livingston Street said: "The house looked desolate, the English ivy and smilax were withering in the rustic hanging baskets, for want of care, and a drooping rosebush sat on the front window-sill." When there was no news, even this was

THE PLOT THICKENS
Reporters following a veiled woman as she leaves Plymouth Church.

fully recorded, in the conversational fashion of the day. "An Interesting Interview with General Tracy," a headline declared:

> A *Sun* reporter called on General Tracy last night and sought an interview with him. It was granted, where-upon the following colloquy took place:
> REPORTER: Are there any new developments in the Beecher case?
> TRACY: Yes, a thousand of them.
> REPORTER: What are they?
> TRACY: I'm not going to tell.
> REPORTER: Why?
> TRACY: Because I don't want to.
> REPORTER: An excellent reason.
> TRACY: I know of none better.
> REPORTER: Good night.
> TRACY: The same to you.

Nonsense limericks were regularly penned, such as these in the *Sun*:

> Said Tilton: The man's pusillanimous,
> And he thinks that I'll knuckle to any muss,
> If he won't let me live
> His confession I'll give
> And then they'll see who's magnanimous.

> Said Beecher: The voice of the nation
> Is loud for an investigation;
> So I'll find me six friends
> Who are pledged to my ends,
> And from them get a full vindication.

One editor commented acidly: "Everybody has made a statement about somebody else. I, thou, he, you, we, they, he, she and it have or hast made statements. There are almost as many statement-makers as there are candidates for the

Vice-Presidency, and they constitute a large proportion of the population." Beecher, who had bemoaned the fact that "everybody in this business seems to have copies of everything except myself," claimed he did not read the statements, even the committee's clearance of him. He did not have to, he told a reporter, adding that "I haven't been down to the shore to look at the waves, but I've heard them roar." With the case taking whole pages, national and world news was often reduced to one or two lines. The Carlist uprisings in Spain and Disraeli's speeches in Parliament were tersely reported. Abroad, the press dealt with the scandal in America more curiously than carefully. *Le Journal de Marseille* called it "*L'affaire Beecher-Stilton, et Victoria Vodull*" and all three were described as members of the Anglican clergy who had been led astray by "Madame Breechestow," said to be "the mother of Uncle Tom."

The contagion spread, accompanied by wild rumors, among them reports that Tilton had shot Beecher. Not only the New York papers but those in other cities reproduced the voluminous evidence as it came out. Special supplements and Sunday sections containing copies of the famous letters in the case, most of them with nicknames by now such as Beecher's "Ragged Edge Letter" (in which he had declared himself to be on "the ragged edge" of despair), were circulated all over the country. The pamphleteers and cartoonists took up the cue. The *Chicago Tribune*, which earned a reputation for honest, probing journalism by the way it handled the Beecher-Tilton case, printed thirty-three columns of the Tiltons' love-letters of 1866–70 to each other, revealing that Beecher's interest in Lib Tilton had been persuasive for some time. The *Tribune* appended its own comment: "The young woman or married woman who finds herself besieged by a Plato, especially a white-cravated one, had better betake herself to the wash-tub, or some other form of labor not conductive to sentiment, if she wishes to be safe." The same paper printed a cogent and critical summary of the case by Elizabeth Cady Stanton, who knew firsthand about Beecher's invasion of the home, and who sadly noted:

THE TRUTH

One of the Vilest Con-
spiracies on Record
Disclosed.

HONEST SORROW TRADED UPON.

A Manly Regard for the Honor of
Women and the Purity of
Children Turned to Profit.

THE BIRTH OF THE SCANDAL.

Theodore Tilton Its Father and
Henry C. Bowen and
Francis D. Moulton
Its Nurses.

MR. BEECHER ON HIMSELF

The Heart of the
Great Preacher
Laid Bare.

FOUR YEARS OF MISERY.

A Story True in Every Line,
Yet Stranger Than
All Fiction.

H. W. B.

Mr. Beecher's Statement and
Cross-Examination Be-
fore the Committee.

A LONG PROMISED STORY.

The Origin and Progress
of the Trouble.

TILTON'S WILD VIEWS.

Gossip, Tattle and Scandal of a Crowd
of Malicious Women.

MOULTON'S POLICY.

Beecher's Claim that It Was
All Paternal.

MRS. TILTON'S CONFESSION.

History of the Visit to Mrs. Tilton's Sick Chamber.

THE ANKLE SCENE LEFT OUT.

Beecher's Endeavors to Reconcile Elizabeth and Theodore.

HIS EXPLANATION OF THE LETTERS.

The Bedroom Scene
Unnoticed.

Tilton and Moulton's Success in Obtaining Money from Beecher.

MOULTON'S PISTOL.

The Plymouth Pastor Writes
His Resignation.

THE QUERY UNANSWERED YET.

The Investigating Committee met yesterday

HEADLINES OF THE DAY

What a holocaust of womanhood we have had in this investigation! What a football the Committee, the lawyers, Mrs. Beecher and her husband have made of Elizabeth R. Tilton! What statements and counter-statements they have wrung from her unwilling lips, then, like a withered flower, 'the Great Preacher' casts her aside and tells the world that she thrust her affections on him unsought—the crowning perfidy in that bill of impeachment that blackens everyone who dared to hear or tell of the most astonishing scandal of the 19th century . . . If the secret history of this tragedy is ever brought to light, we shall have such revelations of diplomacy and hypocrisy in high places as to open the eyes of the people to the impossibility of securing justice for anyone when money can be used against him.

Not to be outdone, two other Chicago papers delved into Beecher's past and came up with the story of his seduction of Lucy Maria Bowen, the first wife of Henry Bowen, the publisher, and of the pastor's still earlier affair of the heart out West with Betty Bates, the teen-age girl. In Indianapolis, Miss Bates's home, the *Sentinel* commented that "artistically, this Beecher-Tilton scandal is the grandest tragedy this generation will ever witness." In Louisville, Henry Waterson, of the *Courier-Journal*, called the evidence of Beecher's guilt "positive, presumptive and overwhelming" and said the deacons of the church, no matter what they did, "cannot restore the fame of the false pastor and the wicked wife." Donn Piatt, a well-known Washington commentator, spoke of Beecher's "stout, burly form full of hot blood and human passion and a face upon which is written in living, unmistakable lines sensualism of the most positive sort."

In New York, however, most of the large papers held fast for the pastor, or nursed a pained neutrality. The *Times*, which eventually was to swing sedately into the opposite camp, looked down its nose at the shenanigans across the river, referring to the case as "this Brooklyn nuisance" and commenting acidly that "Certainly all of these people seem to live in a world of

DISCORD AMONG THE ANGELS

Tilton: "I say you did it!" Beecher: "I say I didn't—what are you going to do about it?"

their own." Beecher's own statement, the paper added, "discloses a curious amount of moral cowardice and a great amount of irrational behavior . . . but we believe the impression will be general that, conceding Mr. Beecher's character to be what he paints it, his story is not inconsistent with innocence." The *Tribune* wrote: "The man at whose door the shameful sin is laid is a clergyman whose name has been honored wherever the English language is spoken. Over sixty years of honest life bear witness for him . . . Unless this frightful exposition is answered promptly and fully, the most famous pulpit the world has seen since Paul preached on the Hill of Mars is silenced, the life of the greatest preacher in the world is ended . . . If not, the pistol shot of Booth caused a national sorrow no deeper and not so hopeless."

It was left to the *World* to hurl the lushest epithets at Tilton. "Mr. Tilton has written himself down a dog," it declared, adding:

> He stands before us now by his own act, naked, shameless, and unabashed. Or rather, he does not stand, for that is the characteristic attitude of manhood, but squats before us, a leering, obscene shape, coprophagous and foul, beslobbering with tears and dramatic self-adulation the letters of the woman he had sworn to love, honor and cherish, and spelling out with gleeful, gloating emphasis to the ribald crowd the syllables of a woman's whispered tenderness to enhance the picture he would paint of his own magnanimous moral beauty and of that woman's wretched lapse of loyalty to him and his great heart. It is simply horrible.

Except for the *Sun* and the *Graphic*, which wrote that "if the arrow of almighty justice rankles in his quivering heart, it is because he has not worn the armor of righteousness under the surplice of the clergyman, but has played the libertine while he has acted the priest," only a few of the less respectable papers in New York and Brooklyn, those the rest called "the Bohemian

ONE BROOKLYN MAN WHO DETERMINES TO FIND HIS
WIFE SAFE WHEN HE COMES HOME FROM BUSINESS

press," were critical of Beecher. Shortly after the preacher's
clerical clearance, a reporter from one of these papers, visiting
Plymouth Church on Sunday, described the scene as "Theology
Bouffee."

"Beecher's Theater was crammed this morning," he noted.
The women were more glowing than ever; "their eyes gleamed
with anticipation of again feasting on the voluptuous countenance of their beloved nest-hider."

The *Staats-Zeitung*, gloomily hoping "something good may
come of it," suggested it might be found "in the removal of
the direct influence of ministers upon family life," and added
that "if a domestic priesthood is indispensable, there is only
one person by whom the function should be exercised—the
husband and father of the family." This sort of opinion generated a vast reaction. Letters poured in, mostly from women,
one of whom typically declared that "If Mrs. Tilton is today a
fallen woman and Mr. Beecher is a fallen man . . . the great and
sad fact does not at all prove that ministers and women ought,

NEW STYLE OF BROOKLYN HAT—FOR BROOKLYN HUSBANDS

from this time forward, be afraid of each other," as "a woman naturally seeks privacy when she wants to talk to anyone about her religious life." A prominent Western opponent of women's rights wrote to the *Chicago Tribune* that Beecher had been "a cup overflowing with precious draughts; millions have drunk from the brim, and been refreshed for duty—shall we break the cup because there is a flaw in it?"

Some female worshippers-from-afar even suggested, without supporting Victoria Woodhull and her theories of free love, that a man of Beecher's stature deserved a mistress or two without having to apologize. But it remained for one of Beecher's older brothers, in a Western pastorate, to make the final point of condonation. How foolish it was to imagine Henry Ward guilty of adultery with "an old married woman" like Mrs. Tilton, he said, for, had his brother wanted an extracurricular mate, "there were plenty of young girls that he could have had, plenty of them."

CHAPTER XII

The furor lasted all summer and fall, and by the time the Beecher-Tilton case came to trial in Brooklyn City Court, on January 11, 1875, many of the facts of the scandal were out. Everyone, however, welcomed the chance to see the full cast of characters in the great passion drama assembled and subjected to the hortatory and compelling talent and wit of some of the ablest lawyers in America. The trial lasted six months, with postponements forced by such opposite extremes of climate as ice on the East River, which precluded counsel from crossing by ferry from Manhattan, and heat that made both lawyers and jurors faint. When the jury gave up in disagreement on the morning of July 2, more than two million words had been spoken or entered as evidence.

Tilton's case was presented without embellishment by a dozen witnesses, of whom the most important were himself, and Frank Moulton and his wife, Emma. Beecher called ninety-five witnesses in his defense. Of them all, he made one of the poorest impressions, and had it not been for the brilliant final argument of William M. Evarts, widely regarded as the ablest advocate of the day, who resembled Henry Clay and was a great orator in his own right, the pastor might not have won the disagreement he and his defenders insisted was tantamount to vindication. The trial was remarkable for the acumen and oratory on both sides, two months alone being taken up by opening and closing statements that are still regarded as classics of their kind. Mere name-calling and character-destruction were raised to high literary and elocutionary levels as attorneys fought bitterly but with arch-politeness. William Fullerton, perhaps the sharpest cross-examiner in the courts, repeatedly trapped Beecher with a combination of persistence and sarcasm, weary patience and sporadic fretfulness. William A. Beach, a quiet, probing, white-haired strategist, when he spoke of Beecher as "this aged, and venerable and

BROOKLYN CITY COURT HOUSE

gifted seducer" and referred to his "insidious and silver tongue which would lure an angel from its paradise," gained his greatest effectiveness from the mild-mannered and almost legalistic way in which he said it. Beecher had five other high-priced lawyers beside Evarts, and Tilton had three.

The proceedings provided the chief entertainment in town. Tickets were black-marketed at five dollars apiece, and as many as three thousand persons a day were turned away, affording near-by saloons a booming business. Prominent politicians, diplomats, and society leaders fought for seats in the courtroom with ordinary curious folk and went without their lunch in order to hold them, or bought sandwiches and soft drinks from vendors. Newspapers assigned as many as ten reporters to the trial. The audience was frequently unruly, having to be silenced by Judge Joseph Neilson for unseemly applauding, hissing, and whispering—there were several arrests for disorderly conduct; all during the trial the principals were stared at through opera glasses, which were also sold in court.

Both Beecher and his wife, Eunice, formidable as ever with her commanding features and snow-white hair that blended with her husband's hanging gray locks, attended regularly, and even when he was not there she came and sat impassively, day in and day out in a black dress, like a raven, in a wooden armchair. Members of the preacher's flock attended loyally. "One might almost have imagined it was a Friday night prayer-meeting, so numerous were the representatives of Plymouth Church," one paper said. In the beginning, bouquets of roses, camellias, and lilies were placed on the table alongside Beecher, and he sometimes held a bunch of violets in his hand and sniffed them. Tilton, who sat alone or with Moulton, also received some flowers. Although neither of the two leading women in the case—Elizabeth Tilton, the declared adulteress, and Victoria Woodhull, the first public accuser—testified, they both made brief, dramatic statements in open court. Mrs. Tilton attended the sessions regularly with friends, listening attentively, and often wet-eyed, as she glanced timidly from Beecher to her husband. The latter wore a constant mask-like expression,

MRS. TILTON AND HER HUSBAND PEEP AT EACH OTHER
IN COURT

but Beecher had all his customary aplomb, off the stand. He quipped with lawyers of both sides, stared at the ceiling frescoes, made occasional notes, smiled at all the jokes, and even laughed merrily with everyone else when in the opening address of the opposition a sermon was quoted which the pastor had delivered twenty years ago on the subject of "The Seducer," in which he had said that "the polished scoundrel" would be punished for his "hellish deed" and that "surely Society will crush him"!

Moulton was the first important witness. Now thirty-eight years old, dressed with studied carelessness down to his loosely combed mustache, he lived up to his reputation as a man of the world by discussing Beecher's adultery with what was described as "the manner of a listless gentleman giving his verdict upon a novel brand of champagne." Moulton was on the stand eleven and a half days, and only occasionally did he go beyond a calm recital of the scandalous facts and show any animosity toward the preacher, who had lately been persuaded by his lawyers to call Moulton a blackguard and a blackmailer. Referring to a conversation he had with a friend in the Produce Exchange,

Moulton at one point expressed his sentiments sharply, yet politely:

> Q: Didn't you tell him that Mr. Beecher was a damned perjurer and a libertine?   A: I don't know whether I told him he was a damned perjurer and a libertine. I may have told him he was a perjurer and a libertine, which he is.

Moulton's close identification with the case from the beginning, and his peculiar role as both oral confidant and keeper of documents, gave him almost total process of recall. Beecher was unable to remember countless events, resorting nearly nine hundred times on the witness stand to various phrases of uncertainty, forgetfulness, or evasion. Moulton was far more definite and held his own through a protracted cross-examination. Dramatic scenes like the first interview with Beecher, when Moulton had summoned the pastor to confront Tilton just after Elizabeth had confessed her sin, and the writing of the famous apology to Tilton, were told with such a combination of vivid detail and straightforward exposition that it was difficult to believe Moulton could

FRANK MOULTON

Answering an easy question and a puzzling one.

be fabricating. Beecher, on the other hand, found himself involved in frequent contradictions, not the least of which concerned his various shifting explanations of the charge Tilton had brought against him and its validity. He denied what the two Moultons and Tilton maintained steadfastly— that he had known the adultery accusation was true from the outset and had in full awareness apologized for it—and he claimed the apology he had given Tilton had been for the much lesser sin of having contributed to the dissension in the household by allowing his visits to stimulate Mrs. Tilton's undue affection.

But the strong language of the letter of apology contradicted Beecher, especially such phrases as "I humble myself before him [Tilton] as I do before my God," "I even wish that I were dead," "I will die before anyone but myself shall be inculpated," and "She [Mrs. Tilton] is guiltless, sinned against, bearing the transgression of another." Moulton was adamant in his insistence that the composition, probably the key exhibit in the case, had been Beecher's own. On cross-examination, he said:

Q: Now, when you began to write this letter, you say Mr. Beecher dictated it?   A: Yes, sir.
Q: Did he dictate all of it?   A: Yes, sir, he dictated all of it.
Q: Did he dictate it sentence by sentence?   A: He did. . .
Q: Did you write all that Mr. Beecher said   A: Every word.

Under ardent cross-examination by Fullerton on the same subject, Beecher, who before the trial had called the apology "a mere string of hints, hastily made by an unpracticed writer," but had also referred to it as "my letter," testified:

Q: Well, did you repeat to him what you expected he would take down?   A: I repeated to him my

sentiments on the topics I thought he would take
down. . .

Q: Well, under the circumstances . . . did you not
want him to record your sentiments in your language? A: No, I did not; that is, I should have
had no objection if he could have recorded it in
my language, but I did not expect that he would
attempt to do it, more than to catch a figure here
and there, or some phrase.

Q: Were you not very anxious that the exact state
of your feelings should be conveyed to Mr.
Tilton? A: I relied upon Mr. Moulton to con-
vey them.

Q: Answer my question. A: I was not anxious that
any phrase or any figure should be conveyed.

Q: Answer my question. A: But that my feeling
should be conveyed, I was glad.

Q: You were very anxious that that should be
done? A: Yes. sir.

Q: And done properly? A: Yes, sir.

Q: And with a view to that end, you said what you
did to Mr. Moulton? A: That was the whole
object of the conversation.

Q: Why didn't you examine the paper to see whether
he had done well what he had undertaken to
do? A: I had relied upon him.

Q: Entirely? A: Entirely.

Beecher's great reliance on Moulton, he insisted, was not
tempered by the fact that he had really just got to know him
a day before. Moulton, he said, was obviously a man to trust.

The preacher's claim that he felt a degree of responsibility for Tilton's being fired from his job as editor of the
Independent, Bowen's religious weekly, was also probed by
Fullerton with respect to what the apology was supposed to
be for:

THE STORY OF THE DAY

Reporters busily preparing copy during Beecher's testimony.

Q: Did you say anything like this? (Reading)—"I ask, through you, Theodore Tilton's forgiveness, and I humble myself before him as I do before my God."?   A: I did not use that expression, sir.

Q: Any expression of that character?   A: I used, generally, a statement of this kind—that I had, for my error and wrong in the matter, humbled myself before my God, and I should not be ashamed to humble myself before Theodore Tilton.

Q: You had discovered your wrong before Mr. Moulton came there on that day, had you?   A: There had been, in—

Q: Had you? Had you?   A: Not in its full extent.

Q: Had you discovered it?   A: I had suspected a part.

Q: Well, you say you *had* humbled yourself before your God, in consequence of the wrong you had done?   A: Yes, sir, I had . . . I had seen enough to be very humble about it. . .

The preacher sought, finally, to take refuge in the declaration that Mrs. Tilton had lied to her husband when she told him that an improper relationship had existed between herself and her pastor, and that, believing her, Tilton had made the charge in all seriousness, but mistakenly, during their famous meeting at Moulton's house on the night of December 30, 1870. But if Tilton had simply been misled by his wife, Beecher was still confronted by his own failure to have made a categorical denial of the charge immediately. At several points during the cross-examination Fullerton hammered away at this:

Q: Was it correct to charge you with making improper solicitations to his wife?   A: If he had the evidence of it, or thought he had, there was no impropriety in charging it upon me.

Q: Well, when this letter was written on the 1st of January, had you made up your mind then whether that charge was written in good faith or in bad faith? A: I supposed that—

Q: Had you made up your mind? A: I was proceeding to tell you, Sir.

Q: Answer my question. You can tell me whether you had made up your mind by simply answering Yes or No. A: . . . In the opening of the conversation [on January 1st, 1871, with Moulton] my mind was inclined to think that I had got myself in a very bad place, and that I had done great injustice to Mr. Tilton; and as the conversation went on and I received from Mr. Moulton light on one and another topic, I became entirely satisfied that I had done a wrong to Mr. Tilton, a—

Q: Now, Mr. Beecher, that is as foreign from my question as anything can possibly be. A: I was coming to it.

Q: Coming to it? A: Yes, Sir.

Q: Well, you start from too far off. (Laughter.) I ask you whether on the 1st of January, at the time of this interview, you had made up your mind whether the charge against you was made in good or in bad faith? . . . A: My conclusion was that Mr. Tilton had reason for making that charge, that he had evidence for it from his wife that justified him in making inquisition and accusing me. . .

Q: How did you think he had come to that conclusion? A: Upon his wife's written statement to him.

Q: You did not believe, then, that that statement was coerced from her, did you? . . . A: Coercion I should consider a degree of violence that never was pretended upon her . . . I had no doubt that it had been procured from her when she was weak and sick, and by persistent inquiry.

Q: And you thought that she had told a falsehood about it to Mr. Tilton, didn't you? A: I certainly did . . .

Q: Then I will ask you again, when you came to that conclusion that Mrs. Tilton had told a falsehood about it, and that Mr. Tilton was acting in good faith in making the charge against you, why didn't you hasten to vindicate yourself to him by telling him that it was untrue? . . . A: I thought I was doing it, Sir.

Beecher added that as "I and Mr. Tilton were not in controversy personally," he had left it to Moulton as "the peacemaker" to "express himself as he thought wisest to Mr. Tilton." But there remained no evidence that he had sought to deny any charge of adultery until at least three years after it was made, and then in a public letter that dealt only vaguely with general "charges and accusations."

Fullerton had a gold-mine for delving into Beecher's conscious and subconscious reactions in the number of guilt-ridden letters the preacher had written, most of them to Moulton. He questioned him intensely about the famous "Ragged Edge"

FULLERTON, TILTON'S COUNSEL, PRESSES A POINT

letter of February 5, 1872, in which Beecher had referred to the "keen suspicion" of "hundreds of thousands of men pressing me" and had offered to resign (write a letter "declinative of further pastorate," as he now explained in court) if "my destruction" would both "save" Tilton and free himself from "the torments of the damned":

> Q: Well, then, what was the keen suspicion?   A: The suspicion that some of them had—of these hundreds and thousands of men.
> Q: Suspicion of what?   A: Suspicion of my moral conduct and character.
> Q: Well, didn't you want to clear up that suspicion?   A: I wanted to have it cured, unquestionably.
> Q: Did you expect to cure it by silence?   A: I did. . .
> Q: What could be worse than a keen suspicion running through your congregation?   A: My life could—could kill that, if I was, Sir, to go right on.
> Q: Then, by silence, and going right on, you meant to leave this keen suspicion afloat through the whole congregation?   A: No, Sir, I meant to make it die.
> Q: Not by contradicting these stories?   A: Not by running after stories.
> Q: Not by telling the truth, as you assert?   A: By not telling a lie, but at the same time not speaking the truth respecting these things. . .
> Q: You preferred, then, as I understand you, to be the subject of keen suspicion rather than defend yourself before the church?   A: . . . I thought that when the charge was made against me that that great church was my smuggling place . . . The point of sacrifice was that I was using that church to save myself by it, and sacrifice Mr. Tilton.

An inkling of what Victoria Woodhull might have meant when she quoted Beecher to the effect of being many years ahead of his church in his beliefs was obtained during the

A SAN FRANCISCO REPORTER AND A BEECHERITE IN COURT

cross-examination when Fullerton forced a strange admission from the pastor. The preacher had just reiterated his guilt over unconsciously having won Mrs. Tilton's affections and having "destroyed her and the household and the man that was at the head of it." Fullerton asked:

> Q: Why could you not go to some relative, or some friend, or some member of the congregation and explain all this thing?   A: I could on condition that it was not exposed to the public. . .
> Q: Could you not trust any member of the congregation?   A: No, Sir.
> Q: Not one?   A: Not one, in the condition of things.
> Q: Well, it is well to know that. . .

If he had indeed been innocent, this lack of trust on the part of a pastor as beloved by his congregation as was Beecher appeared especially strange in view of the earnest appeal made to him by one of his greatest admirers, Mrs. Martha Bradshaw, to whom Tilton had gone to unbare his soul shortly after Elizabeth confessed her sin to him in the summer of 1870. Mrs.

Bradshaw, a leading member of Plymouth Church, had written to Beecher in the fall of 1873, after her three-year silence on the matter had perforce been ended by Beecher's appointment of the church committee to judge him. "God knows that I do not seek an interview from any motives of morbid curiosity," Mrs. Bradshaw had said. It was in this letter that she had begged Beecher to "mitigate" the charge that Tilton had made, "ever so little, if you can," and she had added: "I shall be governed entirely by what you say, for I would part with my right hand sooner than destroy the love and confidence which is reposed in you all over the world." She had also begged the preacher: "Will you see me for a few moments, here or wherever you may appoint?" Beecher, in his reply, which was read in court, had thanked Mrs. Bradshaw profusely but had said that "to be let absolutely alone is the sure and safe remedy," and he had told her: "I know very well that the impulse of affection leads a generous nature to wish to fly to a friend's succor . . . but the best help you can give is to continue to love and trust those who you have always trusted, and to refuse to have any hand in giving mischievous publicity to private affairs, even by allowing them to be discussed in your presence."

Under the careful ministration of Evarts, Beecher was vehement and convincing, if belated, in his denials of any intimacies with Mrs. Tilton. Evarts put the key questions sharply:

Q: During your entire acquaintance with Mrs. Tilton, Mr. Beecher, and up to this month of December, 1870 [the adultery charge covered the period from October, 1868, to December, 1870], had there ever been any undue familiarity between yourself and her?   A: (Emphatically) Never!

Q: Had you at any time, directly or indirectly, solicited improper favors from her as a woman?   A: (Emphatically) Never!

Q: Had you received any improper favors from her?   A: (With great emphasis) It was a thing impossible to me— Never! (Applause.)

HENRY WARD BEECHER ON THE WITNESS STAND

Reporters   H. W. Beecher   Judge Neilson   W. A. Fullerton   Theodore Tilton   W. M. Evarts

Q: Did you ever, during this period, have carnal intercourse, or sexual connection with Mrs. Tilton?   A:
   (With great emphasis and energy) No, sir! Never!

Fullerton did not press the point of sexual intimacy, but
asked:

Q: Were you in the habit of kissing her?   A: I was when
   I had been absent any considerable time . . . I kissed
   her as I would any of my own family.
Q: I beg your pardon. I don't want you to tell me you
   kissed her as you did anybody else. I want to know if
   you kissed her.   A: I did kiss her.
Q: Were you in the habit of kissing her when you went to
   her house in the absence of her husband?   A: Sometimes I did, and sometimes I did not.
Q: Well, what prevented you upon the occasions when
   you did not?   A: It may be that the children were
   there then; it might be that she did not seem in the—
   to greet me in that way.

There were other key witnesses who had seen Beecher's
attentions to Mrs. Tilton. Kate Carey, a wet-nurse in the
Tilton home, who suffered from chronic bronchitis she called
"brownkeetoes," testified that she had seen the preacher and
her employer in some familiar poses. She came down from
the nursery one day, she said, on her way to fetch a glass of
water in the dining-room. "I see her in the back parlor, sitting on Mr. Beecher's knee," she told the court. Later, with
Mrs. Tilton "sitting on his lap," the nurse said she had over-
heard Beecher ask: "How do you feel, Elizabeth?" and Mrs.
Tilton reply: "Dear Father, I feel so-so." Mrs. Carey also said
that Beecher sent Mrs. Tilton "baskets of elegant flowers to
keep around her bed" and that "the servants in the house all
knowed it."
   One of the most embarrassed witnesses was Joseph
Richards, the brother of Elizabeth Tilton, who had introduced

KATE CAREY, THE TILTONS' NURSE, TESTIFYING

her to Tilton when the two men were still in college together. After asking the court to take notice of his "cruel position" and asserting that he was testifying reluctantly because "the lady is my only sister, and I esteem her as we all esteem our sisters," Richards was asked by Fullerton to describe what he saw in the Tilton house "that was exceptional in the character or conduct of Mr. Beecher and your sister." Richards said he had been coming down from upstairs once, as Kate Carey had, and that "I opened the door of the parlor, which was closed, and I saw Mr. Beecher seated in the front room, and Mrs. Tilton making a very hasty motion, and with a highly flushed face, away from the position that Mr. Beecher occupied. It was such a situation as left an indelible impression on my mind . . . in relation to other matters."

Beecher's famous phrase "nest-hiding" came in for some searching examination. Mrs. Tilton had used it in one of the clandestine letters she sent the pastor, calling it one of her "weapons" of affection. On direct examination, Beecher denied it was his creation, but Fullerton was scarcely satisfied, quoting from Beecher's novel, *Norwood*, which the preacher had read aloud to Lib Tilton:

Q: Do you remember, in writing that book, of borrow-
ing from the habit of the bird in hiding its nest a figure to illustrate the way that love might be concealed,
if it were necessary?   A: I do not, Sir.

Q: Do you recollect of describing Mr. and Mrs.
Wentworth [the hero and heroine], and especially
the peculiarities of the lady, in the book?   A: No, I
had forgotten it.

Q: Do you remember using this language? (Reading)
"It would seem as if, while her whole life centered
upon his love, she would hide the precious secret
by flinging over it vines and flowers, by mirth
and raillery, as a bird hides its nest under tufts of
grass . . . as a fence against prying eyes"? Do you
recollect of writing that?   A: I do not, Sir. I have
never read the book since the day it came out of the
press . . .

Q: Won't you be kind enough to explain what you
understood . . . nest-hiding to mean?   A: No, sir,
I cannot.

Beecher tried to quip his way through this aspect of the
cross-examination—in failing to remember another decorative
paragraph from the book, he told Fullerton: "It is beautiful, I
think, whoever wrote it, I am willing to own it." But he was
unable to explain several startling similarities between his own
lush literary figures and the romantic allusions he and Mrs.
Tilton had exchanged. Nor could he satisfactorily explain why
he always wrote Mrs. Tilton when his wife was going out of
town, sending this information, as Fullerton dryly noted, "to
the lady who, you thought, had transferred her affections to
you, and created a great domestic difficulty."

The last-minute attempt of Beecher's attorneys to impute
blackmail to Tilton and Moulton collapsed completely under
Fullerton's relentless examination. "I was fought with actually,
and beaten into the use of that term," Beecher admitted, claiming his lawyers "told me I was green . . . they rubbed it into

MRS. FRANCIS D. MOULTON

me." Finally the pastor said he had had "a fluctuating state of mind" on the question:

> Q: Periodical?   A: Well, not quotidian, exactly; it was fluctuating.
> Q: Did it wax and wane with the moon in any way? (Laughter.)   A: No, I think not, Sir. I more days thought it was not [blackmail] than I did that it was.

A key witness at the trial was Emma Moulton, Frank Moulton's wife. A quiet-spoken, timid woman, unlike her "heathen" husband a devout member of Beecher's church, she gave testimony that was in some ways more damaging than Moulton's or Tilton's because she emerged from the background at the trial, and because the pastor's fall had been such a source of deep private disillusionment to her. Confiding in her as a woman, Beecher had told her, Mrs. Moulton swore: "You are the best friend I have in this world . . . for you, knowing all the truth, knowing that I am guilty, will stand by me. . ." Beecher denied he said it, but standing against him, as usual, was an abundance of his own declarations, including the note to Moulton in which he had said: "Your noble wife, too, has been to me one of God's comforters . . . though sometimes her clear truthfulness has laid me pretty flat." Mrs. Moulton's testimony embraced an account of a discussion she had privately with Beecher on June 2, 1873, and it was so incriminating that the best the defense could do was to deny that it had ever taken place. If anything, she told the story more convincingly on cross-examination:

> He expressed great sorrow for the misery that he had brought upon himself and Mrs. Tilton, and upon everybody connected with the case, but said that he felt that he had thoroughly repented, and that he had been forgiven and that he was better fitted now to preach than ever before . . . After lying on the sofa a little while, he got up and walked up and down the room in a very excited manner, with the tears streaming down his cheeks, and said that he thought it was very hard, after a life of usefulness, to be brought to this fearful end . . . He sat down in the chair. I stood behind him and put my hand on his shoulder, and I said, "Mr. Beecher . . . I will always be your friend . . . I am convinced you can never cover such a crime as this and continue in your pulpit, except through a confession on your part. . ." And he said, "You are always to me like a section of the Day of Judgment." And I said, "Well, I feel a great sympathy for you, but I don't see how you can continue in this sort of life, living a lie . . . I have never heard you preach since I knew the truth that I haven't felt that I was standing by an open grave. I cannot express to you the anguish and the sorrow that it has caused me to know what I have of your life. I believed in you since I was a girl, believed you were the only good man in this world. Now it has destroyed my faith in human nature. I don't believe in anybody." Mr. Beecher was in a very excited condition of mind on that day . . . He told me very positively that he should take his life, and I believed him when he said so. . .

Mrs. Moulton testified that Beecher had been so upset that she had "leaned over and kissed him on the forehead" when he told her: "I have a powder at home on my library table which I have prepared . . . and I shall sink quietly off to sleep, without a struggle, I haven't any desire to live."

In denying this long interview, Beecher swore that what he called Mrs. Moulton's "kiss of inspiration" had taken place three days before. "It seemed to me a holy kiss," he testified, "as I sometimes have seen it in poetry," and he did not return it, because "it was not best, under the circumstances, that she and I should kiss." He kept no poison powders in the house, he said—"the only powder that I know of was in gunpowder upstairs." Fullerton hammered at the pastor's denial that he had called Mrs. Moulton "a section of the Day of Judgment," and Beecher found himself again fighting with his conscience:

Q: I asked you whether you said that, or something akin to it?   A: Well, I said that I did not say that, positively, and that something akin to it, I did not say either.

Q: Now, I ask you whether you will go beyond your best recollection, and say positively that you did not?   A: In regard to something akin, I won't.

Q: Very well, then, I have got it. (Laughter.)   A: Yes, sir.

In spite of Beecher's poor showing on cross-examination—and the testimony of the Moultons and others—the preacher's colossal reputation, the sentimental adulation that had become a kind of permafrost icing around his lushly created personality, were basic factors in the inability of the jurors to reach a conclusion. Subjectively, like so many Americans, the twelve common folk in City Court were unable to believe that he, of all people, could be guilty of a low carnal sin. There were additional circumstances in his favor, however. One was the personality of Theodore Tilton, as it came through more sharply than before at the trial. There was a quality of foolishness about Tilton that detracted from the nobility of spirit he

SAD-FACED AND INTENSE, MRS. TILTON SITS THROUGH TRIAL

occasionally demonstrated. He was a sort of Sancho Panza, more credulous and entertaining than tragic, and he was just the sort of man who might wander around the house at two o'clock in the morning switching pictures from wall to wall and testing various beds for size and softness, as was related by Bessie Turner. Tilton's idealism and radicalism had all the untried, illusory qualities of the emerging utopian concepts he too easily championed, down to the "Communism" of the French Commune, which he proudly supported as representing "the same system of government under which we lived in Brooklyn." There was something gullible in the way Tilton looked, his eager blond handsomeness provoking a feeling that if anyone might be cuckolded it was this soft-eyed, perpetual adolescent, who beat his breast and wrote poems for lovers and children which the defense took delight in reading in court because they were so bad.

While Tilton's testimony about specific events and conversations he had with Beecher and with Beecher and Moulton was convincing, he appeared to have been vulnerable on two counts that surely helped persuade the jury against him. In the first place, he had countervailed his own pledge to himself

and to Beecher to help hush the scandal and had told too
many friends about it, either orally or in letters; the fact that
he did much of this to salve his injured pride and to keep
the record straight in the face of the cooperative attempts
to obfuscate it was not sufficient to convince the jurors that
he had meant no harm. In the second place, despite his con-
tinuous disclaimers, Tilton made no bones about his objec-
tive. When Evarts asked him about the letter he had sent to
Beecher via Henry Bowen, in which Tilton had demanded
Beecher quit his job and get out of town, Tilton did not try
to disguise or temper his aim.

Q: What was your object in sending it; what result did
you expect from sending it?   A: My object was to
strike him right to the heart, Sir.

Q: Now, what result did you expect from thus striking
him right to the heart?   A: That he would be pricked
and wounded as he has been.

Q: And nothing more?   A: Nothing more.

Q: You did not expect that he would be driven from the
pulpit or from Brooklyn?   A: Yes, Sir, I did.

Q: You did?   A: Yes, Sir, and he will, too. (Sensation.)

Unlike his truly debonair co-witness, Tilton enjoyed dra-
matizing himself, even in court. And whatever the relationship
was between him and Victoria Woodhull, it was made to order
for Beecher's counsel to delve into. Mrs. Woodhull herself, of
course, had not helped. Her lecture tours, during which she
had thoroughly capitalized on the scandal, had taken her all the
way to the West Coast and had been an overwhelming success.
The *San Francisco Chronicle* had written that "the announcement that 'The Woodhull' would lecture on the Beecher-Tilton
scandal drew a large concourse of the prurient to Platt's Hall
last night" and had noted the typical comment of a miner in
from Nevada to his neighbor: "They do say as how she's light-
nin' when she really do get warmed up." The more popular
she had become, the less hesitant, and in the public mind her

declaration that she and Tilton had been lovers for more than half a year remained far sharper than her subsequent denial. The fact that she also said she knew Beecher intimately, that "I have stayed with him at his house days and nights . . . I mean no myth," did not ring as true in the preacher's case since, whatever went on between them, Beecher surely did not frequent her house and did not have as much intercourse with her, of whatever kind it was, as Tilton did. Tilton insisted in court, however, that the intercourse had been purely social, though he admitted he had stayed overnight at her house once when they were working on her biography. Evarts tried in vain to pin him down on any actual intimacies:

> Q: . . . Do you remember an occasion during . . . your acquaintance when you went down with her to Coney Island?   A: Yes, Sir.
> Q: And bathed?   A: No, Sir.
> Q: You don't remember the bathing?   A: . . . No, Sir, I was never in the water with her, except in the hot

THE WHITEWASH BRUSH

Benjamin Tracy, Evarts' aide and Beecher's staunch defender, warned that painting Tilton black can't make Beecher white.

JAMES WOODLEY

One of Mrs. Woodhull's servants, testifying about "free love" and the relationship between Woodhull and Tilton.

water in which I have been put these last years. (Laughter.) . . .

Q: I will ask you now this direct question, whether [the] three days, the 3rd, 4th, and 5th of July, 1871, you were not in the company of Mrs. Woodhull, or at her house, and did not spend either those three nights, or one of those nights, at her house?   A: I will answer part of that question, Sir, with a peremptory no; I did not spend either one, or two, or three of those nights; whether or not during those three days I saw her, I cannot at this distance of time say. . .

Q: Then if you had spent those three days in her company, leaving out the nights, that would not have been a salient fact in your intercourse with that lady that would fix itself in your memory?   A: That would have depended entirely on what transpired.

At one point, in the witness chair, Tilton turned to the jury and declared: "I wish distinctly to say . . . that my relationship with Mrs. Woodhull was a wrong one as the event has justified, and I do not ask any man to defend me for it, but to blame me for it." But, he added: "I say here before God that Mr. Beecher is as much responsible for my connection with Mrs. Woodhull as I am myself." The only difference, he said, had been that he had been "less smooth-spoken to her face and less insulting behind her back" than the preacher.

The defense summoned three colored servants of Mrs. Woodhull's to testify about the alleged intimacy between her and Tilton. James Woodley, a former slave, said that Tilton was a constant visitor to the Woodhull home on Murray Hill and to the Broad Street office, and that he saw them "sitting together talking, with their arms around each other," which he thought was "all very natural" after Mrs. Woodhull had explained the meaning of free love to him. Richard Allen Gray, another servant in the house, testified he saw them with their "arms and heads together in a very lover-like manner," while Lucy Ann Giles, a maid, saw Mrs. Woodhull "in her night garment" and Tilton "in his stocking feet." Mrs. Elizabeth La Pierre Palmer, a clairvoyant associate of Mrs. Woodhull's, swore she saw Tilton in "The Woodhull's" bedroom four times, that they embraced and called each other tender names. (Mrs. Palmer created more of a sensation by testifying about spiritualism, relating that her own magnetic powers enabled her to see "from the forehead . . . what is written on the soul of a man or a woman" and to recall the dead with hymns and poems.) In rebuttal, Tilton's lawyers called the chief luminary of Mrs. Woodhull's entourage, the itinerant philosopher and séancer Stephen Pearl Andrews. By showing how many prominent persons supported Mrs. Woodhull, it was hoped to remove some of the curse on her, and Andrews named two dozen famous men who had attended her ectoplasmic sessions, among them Whitelaw Reid, Albert Brisbane, and an impressive number of governors, senators, generals, and business executives. As Andrews kept rattling off the list, the court finally interrupted:

JUDGE NEILSON: I think that will do.
THE WITNESS: I have a shorter list of ladies.
JUDGE NEILSON: I think we will omit the ladies, Sir. Go on.

"TOMMY" SHEARMAN, LEFT, CONFERS WITH
BENJAMIN TRACY

Beecher's lawyers seek to vindicate themselves as much as him.

MR. BEACH: I think we ought to have the names of the ladies, Sir.

JUDGE NEILSON: Very well, the ladies then; let us have them, it won't do much harm.

Andrews thereupon ran off some of Mrs. Woodhull's female supporters, among them Mrs. Stanton, Miss Anthony, Isabella Beecher Hooker, and Mrs. Brisbane. He supported the story that Mrs. Woodhull first heard of the scandal from Mrs. Stanton. As a center for the "radical advanced minds of the day," Andrews concluded, Mrs. Woodhull's salon resembled that of Mme. Roland during the French Revolution, and Tilton, he said, usually occupied a position of "strong dissent" which added to the lively discussion.

Mrs. Woodhull's capacity for keeping a scandal ball rolling became an out-of-court side-show. Tilton's attorneys subpoenaed her three times during the trial, but each time it was decided not to call her because of the risks of cross-examination involved and her unpredictability. Meanwhile, she reveled in her siren's role. "If I would go upon the stand now, I would hurt someone," she announced, with customary modesty and bluntness. Toward the end of the trial, Beecher's attorneys suddenly summoned her, demanding she deliver some letters of Tilton's. Mrs. Woodhull arrived in court, chaste and demure in dress and bearing. Facing Judge Neilson, she said: "I have reason to believe that some of my private letters are in the hands of the defense as well as the prosecution," an ambiguous enough threat that convinced both sides it was too great a risk to subpoena either her or her letters again. She handed a few harmless letters to Shearman, Beecher's friend and lawyer, who told her they were of no use. Mrs. Woodhull calmly took them back, bowed politely to the court, and retired, in an aura as mysterious if not quite so wicked as before. But her story, as given out later, left her relations with both Tilton and Beecher nicely hanging, and still titillating. When she was asked what Beecher and she had talked about during one of their longer meetings, she replied: "We didn't talk about the weather." And while she denied, as she said the servants had implied, that she and Tilton had slept in the same bed for two or three nights, she admitted they had passed a number of relaxed evenings on the roof of the house enjoying "the starlight and the cool breeze." Afterward Mrs. Woodhull became more like a tigress again. She wrote an account in the *Herald* in which she took Tilton sorely to task for having described his relationship with her as "foolish and wrong." Mrs. Woodhull was contemptuous of him now. She called his attempt to make Beecher equally responsible for the liaison "a little schoolboy's sniveling—'He made me do it, if it hadn't been for him I shouldn't have done it,'" and his statement, she said, "ought to make him a laughing stock." Then she added what far too many persons thought, including, no doubt, the jury: "I have said before that I believed Mr. Tilton would make quite a man if he should live to grow up."

Elizabeth Cady Stanton, Tilton's old friend, sided with her own sex when the chips were down. "Theodore Tilton need not have shirked an acknowledgement of his association with Mrs. Woodhull," she wrote in a Newark newspaper. "Victoria Woodhull's acquaintance would be refining to any man . . . Victoria Woodhull has done a work for woman that none of us could have done. She has faced and dared men to call her names that make women shudder, while she chucked principle, like medicine, down their throats."

The figure finally cut by Elizabeth Tilton during the trial was more pathetic. Toward the close of the testimony, Tilton's lawyers astutely offered to withdraw any legal objections to having her take the stand. The offer was quickly declined, on the ostensible grounds that the law prohibited her appearance (which was debatable) and because there was a "grave moral question" as to propriety. Tilton's counsel noted that there was some question as to "how much of the garment of respectability is left," but Judge Neilson said he was "gratified" the issue was not to be forced. Mrs. Tilton herself, however, did force it the

MRS. TILTON APPEALS VAINLY TO BE HEARD IN COURT

following day by suddenly rising from her spectator's seat "like an apparition," as a reporter wrote, and "in a tremulous voice" declaring: "Your honor, I have a communication which I hope your honor will read aloud." Judge Neilson refused the request, but when the letter she had handed him was made public a few days later it created a sensation. Mrs. Tilton said:

> I have been so sensible of the power of my enemies that my soul cries out before you, and the gentlemen of the jury, that they beware how, by a divided verdict, they consign to my children a false and irrevocable stain upon their mother! For five years I have been the victim of circumstances, most cruel and unfortunate; struggling from time to time only for a place to live honorably and truthfully. Released for some months from the *will* by whose power unconsciously I criminated myself again and again, I declare solemnly before you, without fear of man and by faith in God, that I am innocent of the crimes charged against me. I would like to tell my *whole* sad story *truthfully*—to acknowledge the frequent falsehoods wrung from me by compulsion—though at the same time unwilling to reveal the secrets of my married life . . . I assume the entire responsibility of this request, unknown to friend or counsel of either side. . .

In spite of her disavowal, her plea, it was felt, had not been totally unexpected by Beecher's lawyers. And three years later, when she faced her final ordeal of conscience, the letter simply stood as a nice legal maneuver to play upon the sympathies of the weary jurors. There was no denying what Beach, in his summation for Tilton, said: "If she be innocent, if her written and oral declarations are lies, if Mr. Henry Ward Beecher never did address to her base and improper solicitations, aye, if he did not defile her body, that woman thus exalted upon that stand, with a voice that would have penetrated the conscience of the world, could have declared his or her innocence."

WILLIAM M. EVARTS, BEECHER'S CHIEF ATTORNEY

The summations at the trial drew some of the greatest crowds and provoked some of the loudest demonstrations. They consumed twenty-five court days, extending over five weeks, and were contests of classical erudition and oratory as much as they were legal arguments. Freely quoted were Shakespeare, Carlyle, Byron, Scott, Burns, Milton, Dr. Newman, Dr. Johnson, Hawthorne, St. Paul, and the Scriptures. The quotations sometimes ran to thousands of words and were applauded by the audience as if they were stage readings by well-known actors. The theme of good and evil was propounded at length by both Evarts and Beach.

Beecher's choice of Evarts as his chief counsel had been both admirable and wise. There were few jurymen who could not be impressed by William Maxwell Evarts. He had been not only a great lawyer, but a considerable statesman. He had ably defended the notorious forger Monroe Edwards, and during the Civil War he had enhanced his reputation by the manner in which he handled the Savannah privateers and other prize cases.

In the abortive trial of Jefferson Davis for treason, he was government counsel, and he had been President Johnson's eloquent defender in the only impeachment proceedings ever brought against the chief executive of the United States. Johnson had appointed him Attorney General, and he had served as Secretary of State under President Rutherford B. Hayes. He had not only keen legal acumen, but a silver tongue that could cry for respectability. When Evarts pleaded that a victory for Henry Ward Beecher would be a victory for one and all, preserving everything that was "pure" in American life, it mattered less that Beecher might have been guilty beyond a reasonable doubt than that Evarts, in the common man's estimation, was right about the need for such a victory in the face of attacks made against the structure of society by such brazen women as Victoria Woodhull. "Tossed about in endless controversy" arising from the case, he said, were "questions of taste, of social ethics, of manners and morals, of religious forms and religious faith." He adopted a tone of universal defense that was neatly calculated to win a verdict for his client. "Everybody has been trying everybody," he said. "Europe has been trying America. New York has been trying Brooklyn. The other cities and the rest of the country have been trying Brooklyn and

TILTON AND BEECHER
The two principals listening to summations.

New York, coupling them like Herculaneum and Pompeii and Sodom and Gomorrah. All the scoffers and the infidels have been trying all the Christians."

His summation was a plea for "decency" in the best Victorian sense. He particularized it by playing, for all it was worth, upon the great reputation of Henry Ward Beecher, emphasizing the "impossibility" of Beecher's having committed adultery, "the incredibility of so flagrant and heinous an imputation." Evil minds alone were responsible, he cried. "In every quarter where the wicked classes make their meetings, and hold their gossips with a sneer and a smile, the scandal was accepted." To believe it was itself "wicked, wicked as it can be, wicked in heart, wicked in soul, wicked in hate to God, to society, to human nature, wicked in everything . . . Ah! gentlemen, that is the final stage of dissolute immorality in a man, in a city, in a community . . . you have struck a blow not at Mr. Beecher, not at Mrs. Tilton, but at you own wives and your own daughters." Beecher's life was extolled as sufficient proof of his innocence. "You do not need to spend much time in finding out that the scarlet guilt of adultery, and the coarse, selfish purposes of seduction do not match the generous heart and loving kindness, and the nobility of Henry Ward Beecher," Evarts declaimed. "It is a miracle if he was guilty, and you, gentlemen, on the part of the plaintiff . . . must produce sufficient evidence to convince the jury that a miracle has happened in our midst."

In response, with less flamboyance but more pungency, Beach gave some earlier examples of "clerical depravity" and declared that "great and good as Mr. Beecher may have been, he is yet, in the eye of God and in the eye of men, a fallible sinner . . . Are we to have a new version of the Scriptures?" he demanded. "Are we to have new teachings in regard to the fall of man? Are we to be told that there is no sin among the apparently pure and great?" Christianity, he exclaimed, "has stood a great many worse catastrophes than the loss of a man like Henry Ward Beecher . . . There is no fear for the progress of Christian influence. The Church will survive." The real

WAITING FOR THE JURY'S VERDICT
Beecher on "the ragged edge of anxiety and despair."

question, Beach emphasized, "is whether the wealth and influence of Plymouth Church, and the power of a great name, shall overcome the force of proof, the lessons of the law, and the instincts of justice," whether "in his borrowed robes of purity and innocence, from his great position—this potentate of the pulpit—is to overturn all the judgments and all the rules." Tilton was not on trial for his faults, Beach pointed out in answer to Evarts's castigation. "It is no excuse for Henry Ward Beecher that Theodore Tilton was a harsh and unloving husband, if it be true. Even if Tilton was the adorer of Victoria Woodhull . . . was odious and debased in his habits . . . an immoral libertine," Beecher had invaded his home.

In his meticulous charge to the jury, Judge Neilson also warned the jury not to be influenced by extraneous testimony as to Tilton's idiosyncrasies or to be guided by any prior exculpation of Beecher in Plymouth Church. "In any view of the case," the judge said, "you may be disposed to ask why Mr. Beecher, if innocent, should have garnered up in his heart all that pain and fear so long, when he might have made proclamation to the world and trampled out the scandal as with iron boots." It was what almost everyone by now was wondering.

Beecher had gone on preaching throughout the long trial. The evening the case went to the jury, he told his prayer meeting that, no matter what happened, "the world is wide and will not be destitute of opportunities" and that "as long as there is a champion needed for the downtrodden, so long as any need God and they can't see Him directly, they will see Him reflected in me if God gives me the power to go on." He left the next morning for his Peekskill farm, but Mrs. Beecher remained in Brooklyn and kept a steady day-and-night vigil at the courthouse.

The city was sweltering in its first seasonal heat-wave. The crowds congregated in the downtown area, and the saloons were jammed. Many persons slept on the grass in the courthouse square. During its eight days of deliberation the jury did not leave the building, and the twelve small merchants, headed by a flour-dealer, took turns sleeping on a pair of old mattresses a few hours each night. Food, changes of clothing, toilet articles, and drugs were sent into them after careful inspection by Judge Neilson. Several jurors became ill, including the foreman, who got colic and had to be given a tumbler of brandy. The heat increased, and the jurymen began moving from one side of the courthouse at noon to the other. These shifts were followed from rooms and roofs of surrounding buildings, rented out to the curious. Reporters clung to lampposts and crawled out onto window ledges with spyglasses. Diagrams of the jury in various postures of debate were printed and analyzed, and each juror's background was studied. By the sixth night, exhaustion had set in all around. "The jury was extremely quiet last night," a story read. "Its members laid themselves yawningly over the tables and gaped.

THE IDOL AND HIS IDOLATORS

Beecher being given flowers as he boards his White Mountains train.

Half-nakedness is its condition by choice." Judge Neilson was described as "a semi-perambulating sponge."

At 11.17 a.m. on July 2 the jurors dragged themselves into court. After fifty-two ballots, no agreement was possible, they said. At the outset they had been eight to four against a verdict for Tilton, and at the end they stood nine to three against him. Tilton came rushing into the courtroom just as the jurors were being discharged. As soon as Judge Neilson finished, reporters, assigned in groups, went after "the unfortunate twelve." Six men, with pencils flashing, besieged a Tilton holdout. "There was a sweaty glare in their eyes, and a savage quickness in their breath that was ominous of evil to him," it was reported. "He walked quickly along but he could not shake the wild animals." The courtroom was a bedlam. "Gray beards of ordinarily dignified demeanor were frisking from table to table."

What had come to be called "the Plymouth section" gathered around Mrs. Beecher and convoyed her home. Tilton, "looking as calm and as placid as a lake on a summer morning," went out quietly, alone. Mrs. Tilton was at her mother's house, and Beecher, having returned to Brooklyn for his weekly prayer meeting, was in his study on Columbia Heights. When he entered the church that evening, a crowd on the sidewalk cheered. Inside, there was hysterical sobbing as he read the hymn "Christ leads me through no darker rooms than He went through before . . ." On Sunday the crowds were so great that extra police had to be called to keep order on the street. Red and white roses covered the platform, and a burning bush stood alongside. Beecher preached on the language of the New Testament. A few days later he went north, as usual, to his retreat in New Hampshire, where in a corner of Twin Mountain House, with the Golden Rule hanging on a wall, he entertained his "summer parish" by conducting a mock Beecher-Tilton trial.

CHAPTER XIII

Not all of the preacher's real trials, however, were over yet.

Public opinion had swung, led by such conservative spokesmen as the *New York Times*, which ran a detailed analysis of the case and concluded that "there are comparatively few who will not in their hearts be compelled to acknowledge that Mr. Beecher's management of his private friendships and affairs has been entirely unworthy of his name, position and sacred calling." While it was "a mournful sight to see a great preacher resting under even the suspicion of a dark crime," the facts "tell heavily against Mr. Beecher," the *Times* said, pointing out that "every theory which he put forward to account for his conduct *before* the trial was expressly contradicted by himself or his counsel *during* the trial." Tilton was censured for having continued to live with his wife, knowing her guilty, and Elizabeth Tilton was called "degraded and worthless." Accusing her of "constructing a form of religion to suit her own circumstances and desires," the *Times* concluded that "a city full of such women would not be worth the trouble and misery which this one has occasioned." At least, the editors declared hopefully, the trial would "lead people of Brooklyn and those elsewhere to distrust the Gospel of Love and to allow no priests and ministers to come between husband and wife."

THE DANGERS OF PASTORAL AFFECTION

Mrs. Brown: *"Parson, I ain't been to see ye lately, 'cause this 'ere Brooklyn business made me think—if I came too often, folks might talk about us."*

Others were even harsher in their judgments, calling Beecher's creed "the Gospel of Gush." Henry Watterson, of the *Louisville Courier Journal*, now labeled the pastor "a dung-hill covered with flowers." Tom Appleton, a popular commentator, said that "Mankind fell in Adam, and has been falling ever since, but never touched bottom till it got to Henry Ward Beecher." It was "the close of the Beecher dispensation," said the *Chicago Standard*, a Baptist paper, and the *St. Louis Christian Advocate* commented that "the church is about as deep in the mud as the pastor is in the mire."

The furor spread to England. The *Times* of London, incensed at a group of English ministers who sent Beecher their "unabated love" during the trial, declared: "The society amid which Beecher moved in Plymouth Church is evidently one of those eccentricities of humanity which may be quite harmless in a country with so many safety valves as America, but which would run considerable risks, in this country, of offending against the practical view we take of the simpler commandments." The *London Daily Telegraph*, asserting that Beecher had "acted with an imbecility that would have disgraced an uneducated girl," said: "We should bear in mind that [Beecher] has not been convicted of adultery, but he is not the only person in the world entitled to that negative praise." It compared his strange behavior to "the poor little nuns of the middle ages, who used to inflict on themselves painful penances because on Friday they had 'unwillingly' eaten flesh." The *Spectator* spoke of Beecher's peculiar inclination "to be always kissing, pardoning, slobbering, crying and writing hysterical Americanese"; and George Meredith wrote: "Guilty or not guilty, there is a sickly snuffiness about the religious fry that makes the tale of their fornications and adulteries absolutely repulsive to read of . . . it disgusts one more than a chronicle of the amours of costermongers." When "Tearful Tommy" Shearman, the staunch Beecherite, came to England and announced that his idol had at most been guilty of kissing Mrs. Tilton and that he loved him more than any other human, the *Pall Mall Gazette* noted caustically that "when a man holds such sentiments, his jealousy will be aroused when he catches a stranger kissing—not his wife—but his pastor."

In Brooklyn, the Plymouth Church deacons started a fund to raise $100,000 for Beecher's trial expenses, printed copies of Evarts's summation, and sent them to libraries and churches everywhere. But on the sidewalks of Brooklyn Heights, and soon all over the city, youngsters sang little ditties, such as:

PLYMOUTH CHURCH NEARLY BURIED BY SCANDAL WEEDS

Beecher, Beecher is my name,
Beecher till I die!
I never kissed Mis' Tilton,
I never told a lie!

and exchanged sly jokes, until the *New York Tribune* commented: "Ten thousand immoral and obscene novels could not have done the harm which this case has done in teaching the science of wrong to thousands of quick-witted and curious boys and girls." Worst of all for the Beecherites was the threat of further prosecutions. Talk of another trial faded during the summer of 1876, but Beecher had overhastily sued Frank Moulton for criminal libel after the 1874 church-committee hearings. "The Mutual Friend" now clamored to be tried, daring Beecher to prove the adultery charge was untrue. This time, Beecher's lawyers knew, Elizabeth Tilton would be subpoenaed and both she and the pastor would be rigorously cross-examined. "Pulpit or prison," Moulton insisted, but the suit was *nolle prossed.* Moulton thereupon sued Beecher for malicious prosecution, but this indictment, too, over Moulton's howls, was finally dismissed. There was nothing further Beecher could do about him, but when he returned to Brooklyn in the fall he resolved to get rid of any lingering opposition in his church. Emma Moulton was still a church member, and a likely target. Beecher moved to dismiss her from the rolls. Mrs. Moulton demanded she be tried by other than the pastor's chosen judges. She lost, but not before the preacher and his church had been further discredited, in the public eye, for running another "clerical kangaroo court."

In February 1876 more than two hundred Congregationalists and their guests arrived in Brooklyn, all of them on Beecher's invitation, for another Council. Beecher outdid himself. He arranged for Council members to be served special lunches and brochures by liveried church ushers. The Council not only obediently supported his handling of Emma Moulton's case, but suggested the appointment of a five-man "scandal bureau" to handle all fresh rumors about Beecher which kept

POLICE ON DUTY

Scene in church alley during new church council.

cropping up, and to dismiss them once and for all. Before a packed church Beecher cried: "If there be any angel of God, semi-prescient or omniscient, I challenge him to say aught." Then, turning his face upward as the applause welled forth, he shouted: "I challenge the truth from God himself!" Women wept and fluttered their handkerchiefs as Beecher grew suddenly abject. "What's the use?" he asked. "I expect to walk with a clouded head, not understood until I go to heaven, and that is not far off." He paused. "Must I run up and down, hunting every leech, every worm, and every poisonous insect? As long as God Himself knows, and my mother knows, I don't care. . ."

The "scandal bureau" was duly appointed, but no one dared or deigned come before it. When the show was over, the preacher gave another tearful talk. "I have not been pursued as an eagle or a lion," he cried. "I have not even been pursued as wolves or foxes, but I have been pursued as if I was a maggot in a rotten corpse . . . When you shall find a heart to rebuke the twining morning-glory, you may rebuke me for misplaced confidence . . . for loving where I should not love. It is not my choice; it is my necessity. And I have loved on the right and on the left, here and there, and it is my joy that today I am not ashamed of it. I am glad of it . . . " It was the closest Beecher ever came to a confession, except perhaps eight years later in the midst of the campaign to elect Grover Cleveland as President of the United States. When the awful story of Cleveland's illegitimate child came out, Beecher, deeply affected, spoke of "the gloomy night of my own suffering" and of his pledge to help a friend "should a like serpent crush him." Finally, he told a Brooklyn audience that "if every man in New York State tonight who has broken the seventh commandment voted for Cleveland, he would be elected by a 200,000 majority." Cleveland's victory was tantamount to another Council exculpation for Henry Ward Beecher.

Only one man stood up to Beecher after the 1876 Council proceedings. At a special meeting of the Plymouth Church Examining Committee, Henry Bowen, the publisher, who had been responsible for inciting Theodore Tilton to attack Beecher and had then backed away from his pledge to support the attack, was at last led to bring his own charge of having been

HENRY BOWEN, THE PUBLISHER, TESTIFYING

cuckolded by the preacher. But for Bowen it was a swan song, and he knew it. The meeting was jammed, and only ticket-holders could enter; a special police platoon was summoned to keep order. It was only after the jeers in the balcony had died away, and as Beecher stared idly at the ceiling and Eunice Beecher glowered, that the man who had brought Beecher to Brooklyn was able to tell his story.

The pastor of Plymouth Church, Bowen declared, was "an adulterer, a perjurer and a blasphemer." He went on: "I received from a lady whom, under the circumstances, I was compelled to believe . . . full and explicit confessions of adultery with Mr. Beecher . . . For many years I have had absolute knowledge that he is a guilty man. My knowledge is so certain that it can never be shaken by any denials or protestations or oaths, past or future." He mentioned no names, but when he told of a woman to whom the pastor had given a key to his study in the rear of the church, where he had "frequent intercourse" with her, and into which one day, when the affair had ended, she had been shocked to see another woman enter with a key, there was no one in the audience who did not know that Bowen was talking about Lucy Maria Bowen, his first wife, who had died soon after that shock. "The evidence that has come to me in the later case of Mrs. Tilton, and which was not accessible in the trial, is so clear that it is equally certain in my mind," Bowen said. In anticipation of his fate, he had never before sounded so sincere. "If you carry out what I believe is your pre-arranged plan and expel me from the church of which I am the oldest member," he told the brethren, "you will do an act for which God will hold you to account, and which I believe the blindest among you will, before many weeks, see to have been a gross wrong. May God have mercy on Plymouth Church in the ter-rible shock of the disappointment and despair that is before it, and may God have mercy on Henry Ward Beecher." When he had finished, Bowen sat down and waited for the inevitable. On the grounds that he had refused to mention names, and had therefore improperly slandered the preacher, the publisher, like Emma Moulton, was expelled from the church.

TO KNEEL BUT NOT TO PRAY
The ladies now listen at keyholes for fresh gossip.

Despite these victories, Beecher still needed money as well as a hypodermic for his flagging popularity. Once again he hit the lyceum circuit, supporting the working man, civil service, and Russia in the holy war against the Turks. He received between six hundred dollars and a thousand dollars a lecture, but it was not all easy in going. James Pond, his friend and agent, wrote that "often I have seen him on our entering a strange town hooted at by a swarming crowd and greeted with indecent salutations." But Beecher was still Beecher, which meant that he was a great drawing-card, who could lecture on any subject under the sun and still pull a crowd, and whose new aura of sin now made him a stronger attraction than ever. The more he traveled, the more encouraged he actually became, and the more his self-confidence surged back. He made diary jottings of his tour. "Next, Boston. Temple full. Received me with prolonged clapping . . . Ten thousand people couldn't get in . . . Papers next morning with kind notices . . . Cheered and clapped when I entered . . . All wept, and it broke up like a revival meeting." In Louisville, "even Watterson sent for tickets . . . I was in good trim, and for nearly two hours I avenged myself." In Pittsburgh, "the love, the eagerness, the lingering and the longing, have been such as to fill my cup full." In Madison, Wisconsin, "the whole slander is burnt over out here, like a prairie or an old corn-field, and will never lift itself again."

Just at that moment, however, it did lift itself. It is interesting to speculate if Henry Bowen had known what was coming. Since the great trial Elizabeth Tilton had been living in Brooklyn with her mother, supporting herself on a small trust fund and teaching in a private school. The house on Livingston Street was empty. Tilton was living alone in a room on Second Avenue in Manhattan. Lib Tilton seldom, if ever, saw Beecher. On the 13th of April, 1878, after long consultation, she wrote a public letter to her legal adviser. It said:

> A few weeks ago, after long months of mental anguish, I told, as you know, a few friends whom I bitterly deceived, that the charge brought by my husband, of adultery between myself and the Reverend Henry Ward Beecher, was true, and that the lie I had lived so well the last four years had become intolerable to me. That statement I now solemnly re-affirm, and leave the truth to God, to whom I also commit myself, my children, and all who must suffer. I know full well the explanations that will be sought for this acknowledgement: desire to return to my husband, insanity, malice—everything save the true one—my quickened conscience and the sense of what is due the cause of truth and justice. . .
>
> ELIZABETH R. TILTON

The letter was published by virtually every newspaper in the country. It closed, said the *Times*, "one of the most pitiful episodes of human experience." But, the paper cogently added, as long as Henry Ward Beecher had not confessed, his apologists would remain satisfied, and "their implicit faith in his innocence is likely to stand a much ruder test than this." Beecher was up in northern New York, lecturing, when the letter appeared. It brought on a fresh mood of self-preservation. He told reporters that Elizabeth Tilton was an unbalanced clairvoyant, thereby bracketing her with Victoria Woodhull, who had once predicted that Mrs. Tilton would tell the truth, though "it will take a long time." Now Beecher said that Elizabeth used "to grovel in the dust and roll in the gutter, even kissing the feet of those to whom she felt herself under obligation." Or so he was quoted. It marked, at any rate, his final abandonment of her. Her letter caused only a brief sensation. It was not only that she had said so many things in so many different ways, contradicting and re-contradicting herself, but that Beecher's popularity was again on the rise. Nevertheless, when the *Times* said that Mrs. Tilton's letter "can hardly fail to deepen the indignation with which those convinced of Mr. Beecher's guilt regard the spectacle of the gospel of truth and purity being expounded by one who has so flagrantly defied its precepts," there were more readers who understood and agreed than there could possibly have been before the scandal was ventilated.

In the last decade of his life Beecher continued to lecture widely, joining evolution and the abolition of Hell (for the support of which he had once criticized Theodore Tilton) to his list of his subjects, and raising his estimated lifetime income to a million and a quarter dollars. He gave his time and name at random to a variety of causes, even becoming chaplain of a National Guard regiment, and he acquired a hunger for recognition which increased as he grew older. He jumped from one political camp to another, hoping for at least an ambassadorship. He had been for Grant, for Garfield, for Arthur, for and against Cleveland, and then finally for Cleveland again. In the back of his mind, even in his sixties, the preacher had the thought that a deadlock in Republican ranks might lead to the choice of him as a compromise candidate for the Presidency of the United States. When it became apparent that his political star had set, Beecher fell back on promulgating a mystic combination of evolution and "The Kingdom of God." He had come a long way from his Calvinist past. "Man is made to start and not to stop, to go on and on, and up," he preached, "steadily emerging from the controlling power of the physical and animal conditions in which he was born and which enthrall him during his struggle upward, but ever touching higher elements of possibility, and ending in the glorious liberty of the sons of God." He called himself "a cordial Christian evolutionist," but distinguished himself from the "agnostic camp" of Thomas Henry Huxley and Herbert Spencer, though when Spencer came to America, Beecher delivered one of his most eloquent speeches at a dinner for the great English philosopher; Spencer's works, he asserted, "have helped me through a great many difficulties" and "have freed me from superstition, from fears, and from thralls, and made me a citizen of the universe." Spencer, however, hardly returned the compliment. He had helped demolish the legend that Beecher had been chiefly responsible for swinging England to the North during the Civil War, and when he returned to London he never even mentioned the encomiums the pastor of Plymouth Church had heaped upon him. In 1886 Beecher visited England for the first time in twenty-three years, but he spent his time with his evangelical friends. Wherever he preached or lectured he was regarded more curiously than seriously, though the trip was a financial success, bringing in, according to James Pond, the agent, nearly twelve thousand dollars.

Europe soon beckoned another principal in the great scandal, Victoria Woodhull, but it became a more permanent, if originally enforced, visitation. The end of the Beecher-Tilton trial had left "The Woodhull" proud but broke. She was also ill, which may have provoked the strange transformation that began to take place in her, for she suddenly dropped her talk of free love and not only reverted to revivalism but came out for purity, motherhood, and monogamy. Denouncing "the loose system of divorces," she declared "reprehensible" the amount of "promiscuousness that runs riot in the land." She took to lecturing on the Book of Revelation, quoting from the Bible to prove that redemption for sin had to come from women, whose bodies and minds held "the secret of eternal life;" her daughter,

Zulu Maud, offered readings from Shakespeare on the same programs. Although Victoria's marriage to Colonel Blood had never been proved legal, she divorced him anyway, charging adultery with a prostitute. The *Daily Graphic* commented: "The High Priestess of Free Love gets a divorce for infidelity. Look out here, or the religion of unselfishness will tumble down."

When lecturing failed to provide Mrs. Woodhull with enough money, she appealed, in desperation, to old Commodore Vanderbilt for help. But Vanderbilt had also turned to decency; he had given up magnetic healers and spiritualists, and he paid no attention to Victoria's pleas. Nevertheless, it turned out to be the Commodore who saved the day for Victoria Woodhull and for his old flame, Tennie Claflin, even if he did so without knowing, by dying. In his will he left nine tenths of his vast fortune to his son, William. Other members of the family quickly brought a suit, claiming the Commodore had been incompetent; among the things they cited was his queer predilection for the spirit world of Woodhull and Claflin. The two women suddenly left for England in high style, and it was apparent that their passage had been paid by part of the Vanderbilt clan. It was to prove the best break they ever had.

When she arrived in London, Mrs. Woodhull immediately resumed lecturing on "The Human Body the Temple of God," and her first address was attended by John Biddulph Martin, the wealthy son of a London banker. Like Canning Woodhull many years before, Martin fell in love with Victoria on the spot. "If Mrs. Woodhull would marry me, I would certainly make her my wife," he announced. Mrs. Woodhull was willing, but the Martin family was not. The next six years saw the change that had begun in Victoria Woodhull extended to a point where it left her former friends flabbergasted. For Victoria to convince the Martins that she was worth John Biddulph's marrying, she had to establish the fact that she was as decent a woman as any, and she went to the most fantastic extremes to prove it. Ultimately she even denied authorship of the famous Beecher-Tilton article in *Woodhull and Claflin's Weekly* which had broken the scandal open; she now claimed it had been written by Stephen Pearl Andrews, the philosopher in her house, whom she called an "arch blasphemer." Solely to impress the Martins, she re-announced herself a candidate for President and declared she was "supported by English capitalists." When Elizabeth Cady Stanton came to England, Victoria met her secretly and begged the old lady, her former benefactress, to tell the Martins that there had never been anything bad in the character of Victoria Woodhull. Mrs. Stanton was honest to the end of her life and refused to go that far, even if she had written that Victoria's acquaintance would be "refining to any man."

Finally, by patience and wearing the opposition down, Mrs. Woodhull won out. The Martins surrendered, and John Biddulph Martin married Victoria six years after his initial declaration of love. About the same time Tennessee (she had re-adopted the full name) Claflin married an elderly and even wealthier importer, Francis Cook, who later became a baronet. The two women and their spouses settled down to lives of ultra-respectability in England, but their notoriety pursued them, especially as they pursued it by forever attempting the impossible feat of denying that it had existed. During several trips to America, each one of which proved more disastrous than the last, the Martins brought a series of libel suits against Victoria's detractors, who persisted in raking up the fires of her earlier life as rapidly as she sought to douse them.

Victoria Woodhull Martin was not the only figure in the Beecher-Tilton case who had trouble living down what had been done. Theodore Tilton was never forgiven, as one of his friends had warned him he would not be, for having sullied the reputation of Henry Ward Beecher. In New York, Tilton found the going increasingly rough. He earned enough lecturing for a time to send his two daughters to school in Europe, but he finally gave up his career in America and left the country for good in 1883. After traveling through England and Germany he settled in Paris, where he rented a room on the Île Saint-Louis and wrote poetry and romantic novels, including one called *Heart's Ease*. He passed a lot of time playing chess at the Café de la Régence. He was there on March 7, 1887, when

Beecher died in his sleep after an attack of apoplexy back on Columbia Heights. The Mayor declared a public holiday in Brooklyn, and the preacher lay in state in Plymouth Church, banked higher than ever with flowers. Newspaper artists drew the room where he died, and pictured the tremendous crowds that came to see him. Nine tenths of the mourners were women, many of whom held their babies aloft for a first and last glimpse of the pastor. The state legislature adjourned, and fifty thousand persons lined the streets for the funeral procession to GreenWood Cemetery. In Paris, Tilton was playing chess when a reporter told him the news. He stared into space, then continued his game without comment.

Elizabeth Tilton had become a recluse, living with one of her daughters. No newspapers had been allowed in the home, though she had followed her husband's literary output, even having his novels read aloud to her when she went blind. In the last years of her life she joined the Christian Friends, a religious society that was "skeptical as to the motives and influence exerted by regularly organized churches." The Friends gave assurances of final salvation to those who believed in "the atoning sacrifice of Christ," and her acquaintances said "this assurance was the secret of Mrs. Tilton's strength." She died in 1897, and was buried in the same cemetery as Beecher. Her husband, one of whose sisters attended. Mrs. Tilton's small private funeral, lived another ten years. He died of pneumonia in Paris in 1907.

Victoria Woodhull, who was supposed to have had a bad heart, outlived all the great scandal figures by a considerable margin. After a final abortive attempt to reestablish herself as a Presidential candidate in 1892 under the banner of "Victoria Leagues" she and her husband formed, she started a magazine in London called the *Humanitarian*, with Zulu Maud Woodhull as assistant editor. But its "manifestoes" in behalf of "Stirpiculture"—the scientific, extra-marital begetting of children—and other causes sounded dull in England, and after several unsuccessful years the publication was abandoned. Still in constant search of respectability at the same time, Mrs.

Martin made periodic trips to America with her husband, even returning in a fancy carriage to Homer, Ohio, where she had been born, and where, at least, she was received like a dowager.

When Martin died after eighteen years of marriage to Victoria, which had been happy years even when he began to wonder what she had been like before he met her, he left her a fortune of just under two hundred thousand pounds. She retired with it to the Martin estate at Bredon's Norton, in Worcestershire, and here she launched a series of spiritualist salons, which she called the "Manor House Causeries." She also started a "college" for women and a village school, and ran flower shows. When the World War began, she worked in behalf of the Red Cross and tried to start a program for women to labor on the land.

In the last years of her life Victoria Woodhull Martin made what was almost, but not quite, another reversal of form, reverting more to type. She supported a "flapper franchise" for women to have the right to vote at twenty-five, and she took up automobiles, scorching madly around the English countryside in a shiny white car and firing one chauffeur after another for refusing to drive her fast enough. To ward off death, which was the only thing that had ever frightened her, she sat up nights in a large chair. But death caught up with her, with ironic ease, while she was asleep at the age of eighty-nine. The date was June 10, 1927, a month after Charles Augustus Lindbergh flew the Atlantic Ocean in his *Spirit of St. Louis,* making the greatest non-spiritualist flight in history. Victoria Woodhull Martin was said to have been entranced.

McNally Editions reissues books that are not widely known but have stood the test of time, that remain as singular and engaging as when they were written. Available in the US wherever books are sold or by subscription from mcnallyeditions.com.